BE THE WORST YOU CAN BE

† † †
† †
†

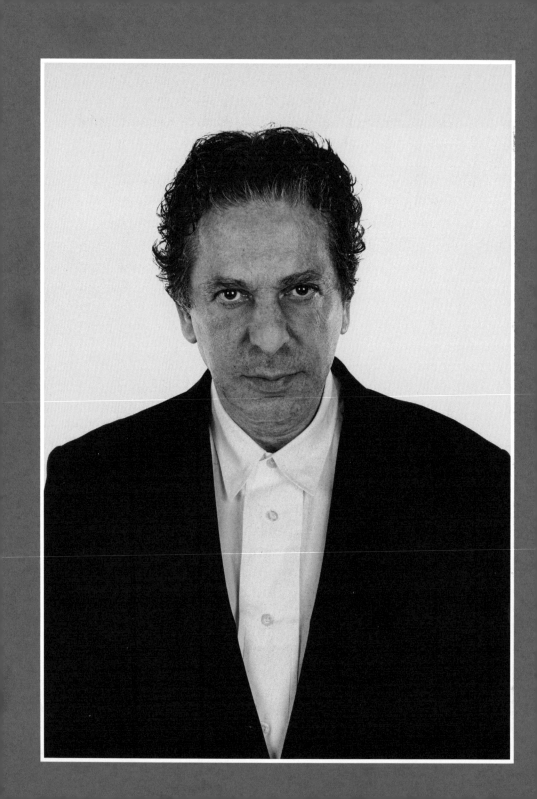

BE THE
WORST YOU
CAN BE

LIFE'S TOO LONG
FOR PATIENCE & VIRTUE

Charles Saatchi answers
questions from journalists and readers

Booth-Clibborn Editions

I FIND MYSELF OFTEN DIS-SATISFIED WITH LIFE AND THOUGH I TRY VERY HARD TO BE POSITIVE I FEEL I COULD DO BETTER AND BE MORE CONTENT AND FUL-FILLED. HOW DO I GET MY-SELF TO SEE THE BRIGHT SIDE OF THINGS?

Are you careful to put other people first? Are you anxious about other people's happiness and well-being? Are you a caring listener and a reliable friend? Are you a sensitive and considerate person?

If you have answered yes to any of the above, I believe we have pinpointed your first mistake. Unlock yourself from the neurotic need to please. It erodes the soul.

You will forever feel not quite good enough. Your worthiness becomes so expected, inevitably your defects become too easily seized upon, and indeed magnified.

Everybody is needy, arrogant, callous, aggrieved, self-absorbed, petty, mean-spirited, spiteful, greedy, envious, ill-mannered and malicious, in some measure, some of the time.

Only when you accept that much of the pleasure of being alive is to enjoy your own horribleness, and the character flaws in everyone around you, will you find harmony and each day will pass more sweetly.

WHAT ARE YOU CONFIDENT ABOUT?

Every day is the dawn of a new error.

PEOPLE IN THE ART WORLD TELL ME THAT YOU HAVE A LIST OF ART DEALERS WHOSE GALLERIES YOU WON'T BUY FROM, WHATEVER IS ON OF-FER. TRUE OR FALSE?

It's not business. It's just personal.

IF YOU HAD A BUMPER STICKER ON YOUR CAR, WHAT WOULD IT BE?

Jesus loves you. But I'm his favourite.

WHEN WERE YOU HAPPIEST?

If you make others believe that you are the cause of their happiness, you can generally feel completely delighted with yourself.

IF YOU HAD TO CHOOSE ONE OF THESE CAREERS, WHICH WOULD YOU PICK: POLITICIAN, TEACHER OR ACCOUNTANT?

I can't manage even basic maths, so possibly I wouldn't make it to the very top of accountancy.

I don't know enough about anything to handle being a schoolmaster, but I suppose I could teach kindergarten children how to smoke.

With a limited skill base, minimal intelligence, and very little numeracy, I obviously stand an excellent chance of achieving high office and acclaim in politics.

DO YOU BELIEVE IN THE TEN COMMANDMENTS?

n overrated lifestyle guide, unsustainable and largely ineffective, only succeeding in making people confused and guilty.

FOR EXAMPLE: You shall not covet your neighbour's wife, nor his house, nor his servant, nor his ox, nor his donkey, nor anything that is your neighbour's.

This was always obviously a no-hoper of a Commandment. Coveting is all everyone does, all the time, everyday. It's what drives the world economy, pushes people to make a go of their lives, so that they can afford the Executive model of their Ford Mondeo to park next to their neighbour's Standard model. And would you want to be married to someone who nobody coveted?

You shall not covet your neighbour's wife, nor his car

DO YOU STILL SMOKE A PACK OF CIGARETTES A DAY?

moking is a dying art. I do my bit to support it. I remember having to write out 500 lines, when caught smoking at school, "Nicotine is an awful curse, it strains the heart and drains the purse." Perhaps that hardened my resolve to enjoy every puff even more fully.

MY MOTHER IS A KLEPTOMANIAC AND CANNOT SEEM TO CONTROL HER COMPULSION, THOUGH SHE HAS BEEN REGULARLY CAUGHT SHOPLIFTING, AND IT IS ONLY THE PSYCHIATRIC REPORTS THAT HAVE STOPPED HER BEING IMPRISONED. SHE HAS SEEN SEVERAL DOCTORS, HYPNOTISTS, COUNSELLORS IN AA-STYLE SUPPORT GROUPS, BUT NOTHING SEEMS TO WORK. AS CONVENTIONAL MEDICAL ADVICE HAS PROVED UNHELPFUL, I THOUGHT YOU MAY HAVE A NEW APPROACH?

orry to hear the experts can't help, but my experience of the problem is nil, so my advice is almost certainly useless.
Even worse, the cause of kleptomania is apparently unknown, though it may have a genetic component.

As you know, kleptomaniacs steal without even needing the things they take, and their motivation is probably different in each case.
Sadly, a recent clinical study at Stanford University School of Medicine failed to find any conclusive benefit from medicating patients with the impulsive stealing disorder. The only advice I can offer is that she carry at all times a letter from her doctor, or hospital, explaining her condition, with £100 in cash to pay for items she has absconded with, hoping that the store will be understanding.
If it were me, I would only let her go shopping accompanied by a friend to keep an eye on her, preferably not a friend who is another kleptomaniac from the support group. Or she could agree to only shop online, and browse the stores with her hands tied ingeniously inside her pockets.

WHY DO PEOPLE THINK I'M RUDE IF I PUT MY ARGUMENTS FORCEFULLY, AND AM STRAIGHTFORWARD IN MY CRITICISM. DON'T YOU DO THE SAME?

sharp tongue does not mean you have a keen mind. If you can't suffer fools easily, be sure you are not one; then you, and others, can be comfortable with your directness.

YOU ARE MEANT TO BE A BIT OF A HERMIT. DO YOU PREFER BEING SOLITARY TO SPENDING TIME WITH OTHERS?

Not at all. I enjoy being with my friends a great deal. When alone I find myself in bad company.

DO YOU BELIEVE IN FATE? OR DO YOU BELIEVE THAT YOUR DESTINY IS CONTROLLED BY YOU? CAN YOU SHAPE THE OUTCOME OF YOUR LIFE?

 do not believe in fate. I do not believe your destiny is controlled by you. I do not believe that you can shape the outcome of your life. People are tossed about in a capricious sea of unknowable, indiscriminate circumstances. Some drown. Some survive. Some thrive.

NOTE

Beethoven's confrontation with fate and destiny is a good example of our ongoing battle with these forces beyond our control. Physically and emotionally abused as a boy, he was extremely introverted as a child and became increasingly isolated from the world as a young man, frustrated by his efforts to earn a living as a musician.

Then, at the age of twenty-eight, just as his music was starting to attract attention, he began to lose his hearing. His first reaction was anger, followed by a deep depression.

"The most beautiful years of my life must pass without accomplishing the promise of my talent and powers," he wrote to his close friend Karl Friedrich Amenda. But six months later, Beethoven had decided "to take Fate by the throat; it shall not wholly overcome me.", even though he was profoundly deaf by the age of 45, twelve years before his death.

It was during this period that he composed his greatest music including the Missa Solemnis, the Ninth Symphony, six string quartets and his final piano sonatas.

Beethoven accepted his fate but he refused to allow it to determine his destiny. Sadly, almost none of us possesses both Beethoven's genius and will, and can do little more than flail about in our sea of circumstance.

The Three Fates
Flemish tapestry c. 1520

Pieter Brueghel the Elder, *The Seven Deadly Sins*, 1558

HOW MANY OF THE SEVEN DEADLY SINS ARE YOU GUILTY OF? PRIDE, SLOTH, ENVY, LUST, ANGER, GREED, GLUTTONY?

✝

All of them.
And they are far from being sins. Rather, they are all very uplifting, and create a balanced and engaged life.

PRIDE   Without it, what is the point of getting up?

SLOTH   Why get up when you can have a nice lie down in front of the TV?

ENVY   Healthy in moderation, forgivable in excess.

LUST   Are you joking?

ANGER   A meltdown a day keeps the doctor away – fact. I read it in the *Daily Mail*, so it is obviously true that losing your temper regularly is an important health aid to avoid stress and heart attacks.

GREED   Hardly a sin unless it turns you into a sex slave trafficker, drug baron or simply a serial mugger.

GLUTTONY   Is right up there with Lust.

ARE WINNERS IN LIFE PEOPLE WHO ALWAYS PUT THEM-SELVES FIRST?

ost of the 'winners' I've met certainly don't put themselves last. And they rarely tend to have low self-esteem issues. As one wife of mine said, "We had a lot in common. I loved him and he loved him." This hasn't stopped my children giving me the 'loser' sign, fingers forming an 'L' on their foreheads as they see me approach.

DID YOU EVER RUN AWAY FROM HOME AS A CHILD?

When I ran away my parents sent me a note saying 'do not come home and all will be forgiven'.

WHY DO BAD THINGS HAPPEN TO GOOD PEOPLE?

ecause our very busy God has better things to worry about than Fair Play, or Justice. Or perhaps He finds good people insufferably smug and self-satisfied. That's why the most horrible men invariably attract the best women. Or maybe because He knows that good people will have a fabulous time of it in the next life.

But I assure you bad things happen to bad people, too. The Curse of Saatchi has never failed, and there is no known antidote. All those who have ever made the mistake of crossing me have been turned into pillars of salt.

IF SOMEONE WERE TO PAY YOU A HUNDRED POUNDS FOR EVERY TIME YOU'D DONE A GOOD DEED IN YOUR LIFE BUT ONLY FIFTY POUNDS EVERY TIME YOU'D DONE SOMETHING BAD – WHICH WOULD MAKE YOU RICHER?

hat a charming notion. All you have to do all day long is be consistently unpleasant, and you'd get paid fifty pounds a time. It would quickly mount up, and even if you avoided doing any good deed whatsoever, you would still get wealthy. This formula seems to have worked admirably for most rich people you meet.

HOW HAVE YOU OVERCOME THE CHALLENGES, AND DEALT WITH THE HURDLES OF LIFE?

Pinning my hopes in their entirety upon St. Jude, Patron Saint of Lost Causes.

HOW WOULD YOU LIKE YOUR OBITUARY TO READ?

Heavily edited.

HAVE YOU EVER BEEN ON A PROTEST MARCH?

I always hope it pours with freezing rain on a protest march, so the marchers can feel more deeply self-satisfied with their humanitarian credentials.

WILL YOU TELL ME A SECRET ABOUT THE ART WORLD THAT WILL MAKE ME FEEL LIKE AN INSIDER?

The Mona Lisa has no eyebrows. It was
the fashion in Renaissance
Florence to shave
them off.

NOTE
Leonardo spent four years on this painting starting in
1503. He never sold it in his lifetime, and it is
still unknown how *La Gioconda*
slipped out of Italian hands
and ended up owned
by French
kings.

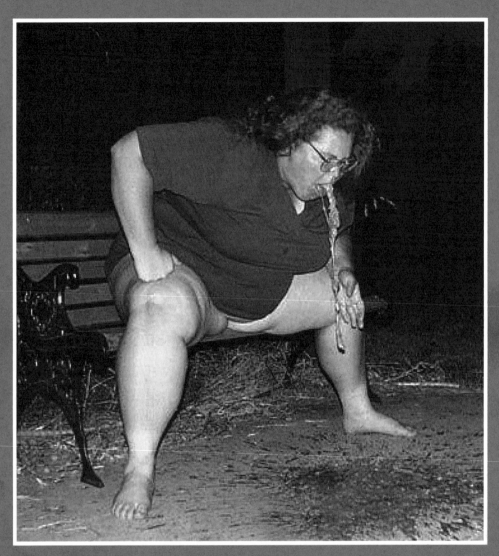

The joys of the Costa del Sol

AS GANDHI ELOQUENTLY OBSERVED ON VENGEFULNESS, "AN EYE FOR AN EYE WOULD LEAVE THE WHOLE WORLD BLIND." DO YOU TAKE PLEASURE IN REVENGE?

f Mahatma had only given me a call before delivering this observation, I would have been happy to set him straight. "An eye for an eye" isn't a demand for barbaric retribution. It was a liberal and measured call demanding that punishment should be proportionate, and fit the crime, e.g. you don't chop off someone's head just for stealing a horse.

As for revenge, of course it is deeply pleasurable. But it can come about in many forms.

Nobody likes burglars, muggers and fraudsters but theirs is a career choice and they are presumably prepared to be incarcerated for their actions if by some small chance they are caught.

We can find a small grain of comfort in the certainty that unpleasant thieves usually end up leading miserable lives, even if they actually believe it will be just lovely living in the Spanish Riviera on the proceeds of their crimes.

Wouldn't you rather have passed away than exist in the Costa del Sol surrounded by the cream of South London gangbangers, with endless rounds of golf and sangria, eating tapas and paella, and going lobster red in the blistering heat, in the company of other unsavoury psychopathic dullards?

HOW DO YOU HANDLE FAILURE?

Very badly. Bitterly. Indignantly. Girly tears. I once saw a 3 hour BBC interview with Orson Welles, and if it is possible to fall for a man, just from seeing him on the telly, Mr. Welles has had me as his love slave since.

Welles had manifold reasons to be bitter about life's setbacks, not the least being that his unquestioned prowess as a filmmaker didn't stop Hollywood treating him like a disease. After years of having to panhandle for backing to fund his film projects, all unwanted by the Studios, all later to be recognized as exquisite jewels, he eventually had to rely on appearing in TV commercials, endorsing wines, or Spanish sherry, to finance his final movies.

Throughout the interview Welles was witty, fascinating, self-deprecating, animated, radiant, sparkling. Without a sullen or bitter bone in his immense body, he was a twinkly-eyed, beguilingly charming giant, not even fractionally undone by the burden of many setbacks and humiliations.

The movie business itself is more than capable of driving anyone quite insane — the more insane the more strangely gifted you may be.

The story of Orson Welles illustrates vividly that it requires a resolutely secure person to take failure gracefully.

Not a hope for most of us, and certainly not me.

NOTE

A quick glance at the history of Oscar winners and nominations throws up many outstanding films that were passed over as Oscar finalists, with more mundane products regularly picking up the plaudits. Since 1950, none of the following movies was even nominated for Best Film:

† North by Northwest
† The African Queen
† Paths of Glory
† Spartacus
† Hud
† What's Up Doc?
† The Manchurian Candidate
† The Big Country
† Scarface
† Vertigo
† Kill Bill
† Parenthood
† Reversal of Fortune
† Harold and Maude
† Being There
† Whatever Happened to Baby Jane
† Lost In America
† Minority Report
† Jurassic Park
† Close Encounters of the Third Kind
† Heat
† Once Upon a Time in America
† Seven
† The Searchers
† Psycho
† Rear Window
† The Producers
† Toy Story
† Apocalypse Now
† A Clockwork Orange
† Some Like It Hot
† 2001: A Space Odyssey
† Lolita
† The Shining
† Touch of Evil
† Gran Torino

† Beetlejuice
† Edward Scissorhands
† Raising Arizona
† Bonnie and Clyde
† Advise and Consent
† Mean Streets
† King of Comedy
† Reservoir Dogs
† Manhattan
† Crimes and Misdemeanors
† Broadway Danny Rose
† Klute
† Spinal Tap
† Princess Bride
† Misery
† When Harry Met Sally
† Sleepless in Seattle
† Bad Day at Black Rock
† Sweet Smell of Success
† An Officer and a Gentleman
† Born Yesterday
† Night of the Hunter
† Planes, Trains and Automobiles
† Badlands
† Three Kings
† Airplane
† Blade Runner
† Cool Hand Luke
† Diner
† True Grit
† The Usual Suspects
† Alien
† Hannibal
† American Gangster
† The Court Jester
† Monster
† Clueless

Orson Welles in a Paul Masson commercial 1978

† The Odd Couple
† Barefoot in the Park
† The Young Lions
† Winchester '73
† The Man
From Laramie
† Hombre
† The Goodbye Girl
† The Day of the Jackal
† Cape Fear
† Anatomy of a Murder
† Serpico
† The Changeling
† East of Eden
† Mrs. Doubtfire
† To Catch a Thief
† Strangers on a Train
† A History of Violence
† Groundhog Day
† The Leopard
† Stand by Me
† Atlantic City
† Body Heat
† Don't Look Now

† Easy Rider
† Rio Bravo
† Thelma and Louise
† Point Blank
† Days of Heaven
† Papillon
† Presumed Innocent
† Run Silent Run Deep
† Seven Days in May
† Imitation of Life
† Miller's Crossing
† Charlie Wilson's War
† The Untouchables
† The Asphalt Jungle
† Full Metal Jacket
† Suddenly Last Summer
† Straw Dogs
† Who Framed
Roger Rabbit?
† Compulsion
† The Accidental Tourist
† The Spy Who Came
in from the Cold
† Goodfellas

Mr. Welles was beaten to an Oscar for *Citizen Kane* in 1942 by *How Green Was My Valley*.

But it would be cruel punishment indeed to the Oscar ceremony, which gives us such toe-curling delight each year, to dwell on the number of times a certifiable dud, like *The Greatest Show on Earth*, beat a masterpiece like *High Noon* to Best Picture.

Of course, you may not agree that some of these films are particularly distinguished. Nonetheless, a list of the films nominated for Best Film over the last sixty years would make the most stoic of men weep.

Sadly, in the movies as in life, being the best you can be isn't necessarily a winning formula.

CAN YOU NAME THE SEVEN HEAVENLY VIRTUES? DO YOU FEEL IT IS IMPORTANT TO BASE OUR PLACE IN SOCIETY AROUND THEM?

A highly important Italian baroque
chastity belt, 16th century

I can name the Seven Heavenly Virtues. They make pretty stagnant fare as a Code of Practice for society.

CHASTITY	Suggests a stolid and antiseptic life. Worthy, but a trifle colourless.
TEMPERANCE	Permanently being sober sounds pretty sombre to me.
CHARITY	Lovely, and nice work for people seeking knighthoods or a sense of self-regard.
KINDNESS	Lovely, but malevolent people are more intriguing.
DILIGENCE	Sounds exhausting.
HUMILITY	Why?
PATIENCE	If it's worth waiting for, it's not worth having.

Pieter Bruegel the Elder,
The Seven Virtues – Temperance, 1560

DO YOU BELIEVE IN MIRACLES?

'm somebody who left school with 2 'O' levels, drove a delivery van in Willesden, worked in a packaging plant in Brooklyn, as a busboy in a bar in New York, petrol pump attendant in Missouri, telesales and then shoe shop salesman in Los Angeles, and a voucher clerk in a small London advertising firm, after being rejected for an interview by all 10 of London's top agencies...

Oh yes, I do believe in miracles.

Smokey Robinson and the Miracles I definitely believe in.

I LOVE THIS QUOTE FROM BARONESS ORCZY, "AN APOLOGY? BAH! DISGUSTING! COWARDLY! BENEATH THE DIGNITY OF ANY GENTLEMAN, HOWEVER WRONG HE MIGHT BE." ARE YOU GOOD AT APOLOGIZING?

Portrait of Baroness Emma Orczy
by Bassano

Very good. And often with no sincerity whatsoever. If you can practise apologising until you become utterly convincing, everyone's happy. You, because you have made life more harmonious with minimum effort. The recipient of the apology, because he feels vindicated and superior. There is absolutely no shame in an apology made with your fingers crossed behind your back, and it is actually quite elevating.

SHOULD EUTHANASIA BE LEGALIZED?
It should be mandatory for many people in the art world.

HOW MANY WOMEN HAVE YOU SLEPT WITH?
None who wouldn't deny it.

YOU STRIKE ME AS AN IMPATIENT PERSON. ARE YOU?
Everything comes to those who wait, but it's usually been left by those who didn't.

I AM THE FATHER OF TEENAGE CHILDREN, LIKE YOU ARE. HOW DO YOU STOP YOURSELF SPOILING THEM?

hy not spoil them, and thoroughly? The notion that children shouldn't be provided with every available pleasure at all times, that an excess of gratification creates unrealistic expectation, that the rest of their lives cannot match up – that is hard to argue with. So why bother? A pampered child will be able to look back at a childhood of warmth and pleasure. Even if later years are less delightful by comparison, the first 20 years will have provided them with many pleasing memories.
Most children are able to work out your efforts are simply a means of trying to buy their love, put you down as an easy mark whom they can readily take advantage of, until something better or more enticing turns up.
My parents certainly indulged my every whim, and look what a thoroughly decent chap I've turned out, a great humanitarian and a charming companion to a couple of wives, who for some reason divorced me...

NOTE
I have sat through four visits to The Lion King, and watched The Little Mermaid on seven occasions, in a fruitless effort to bond with my children.

WITH YOUR TRACK RECORD OF TWO DIVORCES, WHAT ADVICE WOULD YOU GIVE A FRIEND WHOSE MARRIAGE IS IN DIFFICULTY?
Wives make excellent housekeepers. They always manage to keep the house. Boom boom!

WHAT IS MORE POWERFUL –
MONEY OR KNOWLEDGE?

With lots of money in your wallet, you are wise, you
are beautiful, and you can sing as well. But if
you want to know what God thinks
about money, look at the
people he gives
it to.

Money: apparently, it can buy happiness

ARE YOU SUPERSTITIOUS?
I am just a little bit superstitious and firmly
believe in all these words of wisdom,
and a few dozen
others.

†

I   A bird in the house is a sign of a death.

II   A loaf of bread should never be turned upside down after a slice has been cut from it.

III   Never take a broom along when you move house. Throw it out and buy a new one.

IV   If the first butterfly you see in the year is white, you will have good luck all year.

V   If a black cat walks towards you, it brings good fortune, but if it walks away, it takes the good luck with it.

VI   An acorn at the window will keep lightning out.

VII   A dog howling at night when someone in the house is sick is a bad omen.

VIII   It's bad luck to leave a house through a different door than the one used to come into it.

IX   A horseshoe hung in the bedroom will keep nightmares away.

X   If you catch a falling leaf on the first day of autumn you will not catch a cold all winter.

XI   If a mirror in the house falls and breaks by itself, someone in the house will die soon.

XII   Dropping an umbrella on the floor means that there will be a murder in the house.

XIII   All windows should be opened at the moment of death so that the soul can leave.

XIV   If the groom drops the wedding band during the ceremony, the marriage is doomed.

XV   To dream of a lizard is a sign that you have a secret enemy.

XVI   If a friend gives you a knife, you should give him a coin, or your friendship will soon be broken.

XVII   You should never start a trip on Friday or you will meet misfortune.

XVIII   If you dream of running it is a sign of a big change in your life.

XIX   If a clock which has not been working suddenly chimes, there will be a death in the family.

XX   If you believe in twenty superstitions, you will have a very vexed existence.

Not black, but still unfortunate
to have it cross your path

HOW DO YOU REGARD MONEY? IS IT CENTRAL TO YOUR BEING?

People who chase after money, they are avaricious.

~

If they want to hang on to their money,
they are miserly.

~

If they want to spend it freely,
they are wastrels.

~

If they can't seem to make much money,
they are washouts.

~

If they don't keep trying to make money,
they lack ambition.

~

If they get it without working for it,
they are parasites.

~

If they accumulate it after a lifetime's
hard work, then they are fools who never
got much out of life.

HOW DO YOU FACE UP TO YOUR DEATH GETTING EVER CLOSER NOW THAT YOU ARE 67?
People who have lived life fully are more fully prepared for death; you only fear death if you've feared life, he whimpered as he was wheeled away.

DO YOU BELIEVE IN KARMA? HAS ANYTHING EVER COME BACK TO BITE YOU AS A RESULT OF SOMETHING BAD YOU'VE DONE?
I am covered from head to toe in Karma bites, but people like me learn to live with it.

DOES GOD EXIST?

I hope not, as I have blasphemed regularly, always thought Him arrogant and overbearing, with a misguided perception of justice, an insatiable despair for adulation, and profoundly controlling.

IS THERE ANYTHING YOU STRIVE FOR IN LIFE?

I wish to live to 150, every inch of my body functioning in perfect condition, with a nice group of vibrant new friends for whenever my present ones get clapped-out as I stride through my 90's, and I would like to be widely adored by many great-great-grandchildren.

DO YOU READ YOUR REVIEWS, AND TAKE IT PERSONALLY IF THEY'RE NEGATIVE?

I have an idiosyncratic relationship with reviews. If they're approving, I fear that the exhibition must be pedestrian. If they're disobliging, I feel for the critic, who is clearly unenlightened about contemporary art, insecure about a lack of visual perceptiveness, a crabby soul, for whom it would be a kindness to cut short a morose, sour life. A perfectly balanced perspective, as you can see.

WHICH HUMAN BEING HAS DONE THE MOST GOOD?

I am Phillips, founder of Sun Records in 1952 in Memphis Tennessee. Discovered Elvis Presley, Johnny Cash, Jerry Lee Lewis, Carl Perkins, Roy Orbison, Charlie Rich, Conway Twitty.

I FIND IT REALLY HARD TO GET MOTIVATED AND STRUGGLE TO FIND ANY AMBITION IN LIFE. I WORK REALLY HARD AND I DO LIKE MY JOB BUT FEEL I DON'T DO ENOUGH IN THE WAY OF SELF-IMPROVEMENT AND DON'T STRIVE FOR SOMETHING MORE IN MY LIFE. I JUST ACCEPT THINGS THAT COME MY WAY. WHAT IS THE DRIVING FORCE BEHIND EVERYTHING YOU DO?

There is no good reason to live your days burning with ambition. Many ambitious people endure frustrated, unfulfilled lives, forever seeking something 'better', and are overwhelmed trying to overachieve. They would be much happier being less driven. Life is more pleasant without asking too many questions of yourself, or seeking a higher purpose.

A good place to start saving the planet

YOU DON'T SEEM TO HAVE MUCH OF A SOCIAL CONSCIENCE. SHOULDN'T PRIVILEGED PEOPLE LIKE YOU ACTUALLY DO SOMETHING USEFUL TO MAKE THE WORLD A BETTER PLACE?

rying to make the world a better place is usually the province of those who want to feel good about themselves. Caring people do occasionally improve things, but sadly, History shows that do-gooders often wreak as much havoc as the most malignant minds.

So I may be a disappointing person in many ways, but at least I have never fostered grand designs for social engineering, so beloved of concerned types who want to shape the world, and who mostly just mess up people's lives.

Meaning well is not the same as doing good. For example, if you were a local councillor, burning with a desire to save the planet, wouldn't it be better to start by concentrating on having the lifts on the local estate working, and not stinking of urine? Or ensuring that lightbulbs in estate corridors and stairwells get renewed occasionally, in an effort to make them less gloomy and menacing? You would surely like your constituents to be less fearful of walking around the neighbourhood, hoping not to run into gangs of dumbscum, or tread in piles of vomit or hypodermics or broken bottles.

You would hopefully get round to little projects like these before you set about polishing your Green credentials by obliging everybody to separate their rubbish appropriately, under the threat of a £1,000 fine for miscreants.

Saving the planet is all well and good but if people are really concerned with making the world a better place, a good start would be having less grandiose aims and lofty ambitions. More humdrum perhaps, but truly more useful.

WHAT MAKES YOU CRY?

would dearly love to claim it would be a deeply moving piece by Brahms, or a heartbreaking last chapter in a great work of literature, or the cruelties of the world suffered by innocents, or simply hammering my thumb instead of the nail. I am sorry to say I'm not often teary. I blubber like a baby when I do cry however, but my wailing is probably just a result of having my vanity punctured by some slight or other.

WHAT IS YOUR GOLDEN RULE?

Don't wear gold unless you are a blingtastic rap star, in which case appearing vulgar and showy is part of your charm.

DO YOU GET DEPRESSED REGULARLY, RARELY, NEVER?

Never. Rarely. Regularly.

WHAT CAN ADULTS LEARN FROM THE YOUNG PEOPLE OF TODAY?

Do infants enjoy infancy as much as adults enjoy adultery?

SHOULD WE WAIT UNTIL 5PM BEFORE HAVING THE FIRST DRINK OF THE DAY, OR SHOULD YOU HAVE A DRINK WHENEVER YOU HAPPEN TO WANT IT?

Never, ever, delay any opportunity to derive pleasure, for even a second. As the French say, all things in moderation, including moderation.

DO YOU WRITE ALL YOUR ANSWERS PERSONALLY OR EMPLOY A TEAM OF COPYWRITERS? IF THE LATTER, AS I'M AN AGED CREATIVE SIDELINED BY A GENERATION OF MEDIA STUDIES GRADUATES WHO COULDN'T EVEN SELL THEIR SOULS TO THE DEVIL, COULD YOU GIVE ME A JOB?

too, am an aged Creative, and with little to do except respond to these questions. Surely you have deduced from the quality of the answers that no bona fide writers were involved at any stage.

DO ALIENS EXIST?

I was always convinced that *Alien*, made by Ridley Scott, was a documentary.

HAVE YOU ALWAYS STUCK TO THE MAXIM "BE NICE TO PEOPLE ON THE WAY UP, BECAUSE YOU'LL MEET THE SAME PEOPLE ON THE WAY DOWN".

If you're one of those Gordon Gekko types who thinks this is girly nonsense – there's no way you're ever going down – best move on to the next question. The rest of us know that success is 50% luck and the other 50% being lucky in riding your luck.

In general, it is good to be helpful and kindly but don't give yourself to be melted into candle grease for the benefit of the tallow trade, George Eliot said.

There's nothing wrong with being nice to people when you don't have to be. It makes you feel saintly and smug – perfectly pleasant emotions. If being nasty to people paid dividends, it would render the maxim above worth paying attention to.

But we know that bullies often justify unkind behaviour by claiming that in order to make people do better, first you have to make them feel worse. Think of the last time you were humiliated or treated unfairly – did you feel like co-operating or doing better?

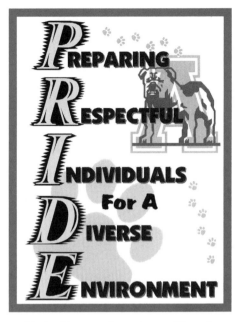

The inspiring motto for students at Albemarle High School, North Carolina

IF YOU HAD A MOTTO WHAT WOULD IT BE?

What is the point of a motto? You will inevitably let yourself down if it's an Inspirational motto. If it's a simple call for Extra Effort, you will quickly get irritated by the constant prodding. If it's a motto that inspires Kindness and Good Works you will forever be haunted by guilt. Leave mottos to other people who enjoy carrying a burden throughout their lives.

DOES MONEY BUY HAPPINESS?

It's certainly true that when I've seen a man get rich, his next ambition is to get richer.

DO YOU EVER THINK ABOUT SUICIDE?

†

 often think about the least terrifying way to top yourself. I wouldn't use pills, in case they leave you alive, but brain-damaged. Too cissy to attempt wrist-slashing or self-lynching. And sitting in a car with a tube from the exhaust pipe, slowly expiring from gasoline fumes, is likely to provide you with a nauseous last few minutes.

I have decided that hurling myself from a very tall skyscraper would achieve the certainty of an instant exit, with no pain, and a particularly exhilarating free-fall fairground-ride demise, as close as I will ever get to fulfilling my fantasy of being able to fly.

NOTE

It would be considerate to ensure you don't land on a car, or someone strolling below; avoid litter penalties by employing a clean-up team to mop up your mess and bin-bag you appropri-ately.

The Suicide of Dorothy Hale
by Frida Kahlo, 1938

WHAT CHARACTER TRAITS IN OTHER PEOPLE DO YOU FIND
UNPLEASANT? WHAT TYPE OF PERSON DO YOU MOST DISLIKE?
As I have suggested earlier, malevolent people are more intriguing, and there
is much pleasure in enjoying the character flaws of everyone around you. The
devil gets the best tunes, so whether it's Bond villains, fairytale wicked step-
mothers or Mafiosi mobsters, the baddies are reliably more memorable than
the leading actors, and the more creepily sinister they are, the more captivating.

I

IV

II

V

III

VI

I   Maleficent in *Sleeping Beauty*
II   Cruella De Vil in *101 Dalmatians*
III   Captain Hook in *Peter Pan*
IV   Cinderella's stepmother
V   Shere Khan in *The Jungle Book*
VI   Scar in *The Lion King*
VII   The Queen in *Snow White*

VIII   Ursula in *The Little Mermaid*
IX   Gaston in *Beauty and the Beast*
X   Jafar in *Aladdin*
XI   Judge Claude Frollo in *The Hunchback of Notre Dame*
XII   Governor Ratcliffe in *Pocahontas*

VII

X

VIII

XI

IX

XII

IS THERE ART ON OTHER PLANETS?

When I first encountered Minimal Art in New York in the late 1960's, Sol LeWitt's conceptual structures, Carl Andre's metal floor plates, Donald Judd's galvanized steel boxes, I remember having the romantic notion that this is what art would look like in a highly-advanced distant galaxy. The work appeared so far removed from all previous earthly art, it was easy to fantasize about cerebral Venusians floating ethereally above a work by Judd, and enjoying its rigorous beauty much as we would admire a Michelangelo.

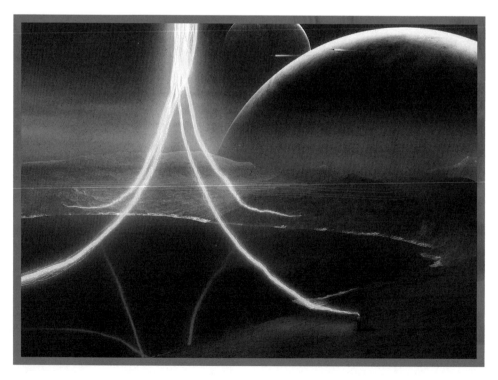

A light installation on a parallel universe created by their Dan Flavin

DOES THE WELFARE SYSTEM REALLY HELP?
Obviously, if you're short on good luck.

NOTE
There are enough painfully plodding books on just this subject, if you wish to analyze the benefits and drawbacks of a welfare-based state. I have a number of interesting views that... zzzz

SHOULD DRUGS BE LEGALIZED?

 aving only taken a single puff of a marijuana cigarette 30 years ago, I am possibly the wrong person to ask.

I do have views, predictably. Heroin is clearly a marvellous product, as it is so widely admired by satisfied customers all around the world.

I can't be doing with hypodermics, track marks or the heated spoon paraphernalia, but if heroin could be offered in more convenient capsule or liquid form, and be easily available at Marks & Spencer or Waitrose, that would be a considerable boon.

As my last years are likely to be crippled with arthritis, dementia, emphysema and heaven knows what else, the prospect of idling away my decline in blissful serenity makes a long life sound quite appealing.

Alongside a few like-minded friends, I am looking for a large home somewhere to establish our commune for aged would-be smack heads. It will be very wheelchair-friendly, with many kind nurses to maintain and feed us, change channels on our large plasma screens, and keep us permanently euphoric on Tesco own-brand Freebase Delight.

SHOULD WE ARTIFICIALLY CREATE LIFE?
What is wrong with the more congenial, traditional method?

NOTE
Nothing against cloned sheep or cows. But if scientists wish to play God, why not put their energies into a more useful project, like cloning hundreds of efficient, reasonably-priced plumbers.

WHAT IS THE BEST HORROR MOVIE?

 eleb Big Brother, which is slightly more horrifying than Pleb Big Brother. Granted, I have only been bold enough to watch a few minutes of either, but they both seem far scarier than *The Texas Chainsaw Massacre*, and certainly more ghoulish.

WHO IS THE BEST SUPER-HERO? SUPERMAN, BATMAN OR SPIDERMAN?
Winston Churchill. George Best. Jackson Pollock.

IF ONE OF YOUR ENEMIES DIES, WHAT'S THE POLITE WAY OF ANSWERING QUESTIONS ABOUT IT?

I did not attend his funeral, but I wrote a nice note saying I approved of it.

WHAT IS THE MEANING OF LIFE?

God knows.

DO YOU BELIEVE IN LOVE AT FIRST SIGHT?

It is possible, but it pays to take a second look. Love may indeed be blind, but marriage is often an eye-opener.
I go along with my favourite philosopher, Cher: "The trouble with some women is that they get all excited about nothing – and then marry him".

Cher Guevara

DO YOU BELIEVE THAT LITTLE WHITE LIES ARE OK IN SOME SITUATIONS?

 nce you start telling little white lies, you soon go colour blind. In any event, half a truth is still a whole lie. I take the Crisp view. Of course I lie to people. But I lie altruistically – for our mutual good. The lie is the basic building block of good manners. That may seem mildly shocking to a moralist – but then what isn't?

YOUR AD AGENCY ETHOS USED TO BE "NOTHING IS IMPOSSIBLE". THIS IS OBVIOUSLY NONSENSE, SO WHY DID YOU USE IT?

 always liked John Andrew Holme's view: Never tell a young person that anything cannot be done. God may have been waiting centuries for someone ignorant enough of the impossible to do that very thing.

ARE YOU PATIENT DRIVING BEHIND A SLOW-MOVING CAR IN FRONT OF YOU?

Pass.

SHOULD CREATIONISM BE TAUGHT IN SCHOOLS?

Not taught. Discussed.

IN JACK GARDNER'S BOOK, 'WORDS ARE NOT THINGS,' HE WRITES, 'WE CHOOSE THE MORALITY THAT SUITS OUR AMBITIONS.' IS THIS WHY SAATCHI & SAATCHI BECAME SO SUCCESSFUL?

The Executive Smoking Room in our Manila branch

ny suggestion that advertising agencies are less than scrupulously ethical is wholly inaccurate and most distressing. I have never known anybody in the advertising industry who is not guided by a strict moral compass, who is not resolute in maintaining the highest principles at all times, who does not strictly adhere to all teachings of the Bible. Thank you for your interest.

DO YOU OFTEN THINK ABOUT DYING?

We all die, but not all of us live. On your deathbed, when your life flashes before your eyes, it should be worth watching. Wouldn't you rather burn out than fade away? (cue soaring heavy metal guitar solo).

Laurence Olivier in *Hamlet*

NOTE

Without wanting to appear morbid, I have a little collection of Famous Last Words; here are my favourites should you care to share this dubious pleasure.

LOUIS XIV
(1638–1715)
Why are you weeping? Did
you imagine that I was immortal?
To his attendants who were crying.

SALVADOR DALÍ
(1904–1989)
Where is my clock?

ALDOUS HUXLEY
(1894–1963)
LSD, 100 micrograms I.M.
*To his wife. She obliged and he was
injected twice before his death.*

THOMAS J. GRASSO
(D. 1995)
I did not get my Spaghetti–O's,
I got spaghetti. I want the press
to know this.
Executed by injection, Oklahoma.

JOAN CRAWFORD
(1905–1977)
Dammit... Don't you dare ask God
to help me.
*To her housekeeper who began to
pray aloud.*

LADY NANCY ASTOR
(1879–1964)
Jakie, is it my birthday or am I dying?
*Seeing all her children assembled
at her bedside.*

LAURENCE OLIVIER
(1907–1989)
This isn't Hamlet, you know. It's not
meant to go into the bloody ear.
*Said this when a nurse, attempting to
moisten his lips, mis-aimed.*

P. T. BARNUM
(1810–1891)
[American showman]
How were the receipts today at
Madison Square Garden?

MARVIN GAYE
(1939–1984)
Mother, I'm going to get my things
and get out of this house. Father
hates me and I'm never coming back.
*Moments later, Gaye was fatally shot
by his father, Marvin Gaye, Sr.*

GEORGE BERNARD SHAW
(1856–1950)
Dying is easy, comedy is hard.

WYNDHAM LEWIS
(1884–1957)
Mind your own business.
*When his nurse asked him about the
state of his bowels on his deathbed.*

KING GEORGE V OF THE UNITED KINGDOM
(1865–1936)
Bugger Bognor.
*His physician had suggested that he re-
lax at his seaside palace in Bognor Regis.*

JOSEPH HENRY GREEN
(1791–1863)
It's stopped.
Upon checking his own pulse.

GEORG FRIEDRICH WILHELM HEGEL
(1770–1831)
Only you have ever understood me.
...And you got it wrong.
To his favourite student.

Oscar Wilde and the offending wallpaper

OSCAR WILDE
(1854 – 1900)
Either this wallpaper goes, or I do.

SAKI
(1870 – 1916)
Put that bloody cigarette out.
To a fellow officer while in a trench during World War One, for fear the smoke would give away their positions. He was then shot by a German sniper who had heard the remark.

JAMES W. RODGERS
(1910 – 1960)
[American criminal]
Why yes, a bulletproof vest.
On his final request before the firing squad.

HUMPHREY BOGART
(1899 – 1957)
I should never have switched from Scotch to Martinis.

VOLTAIRE
(1694 – 1778)
This is no time to make new enemies.
When asked on his deathbed to forswear Satan.

BING CROSBY
(1903 – 1977)
That was a great game of golf, fellas.

JOHN SEDGWICK
(1813 – 1864)
Nonsense, they couldn't hit an elephant at this distance.
In response to a suggestion that he should not show himself over the parapet during the Battle of the Wilderness.

TERRY ALAN KATH
(1946 – 1978)
[Founding member of the rock band Chicago]
Don't worry, it's not loaded.
Playing with a gun, the single bullet left in the chamber killed him instantly.

PAUL CLAUDEL
(1868 – 1955)
Doctor, do you think it could have been the sausage?

VIC MORROW
(1929 – 1982)
I should have asked for a stunt double.
Morrow said this before filming a challenging scene for 'Twilight Zone: The Movie' with a helicopter which lost control.

GOOD NEWS
THEIR MAJESTIES THE KING & QUEEN
AT BOGNOR

The Death of Voltaire
Late 18th century wax relief, Samuel Percy

HOW DO YOU FEEL ABOUT WOMEN SPENDING £1000 ON A PAIR OF SHOES OR £2000 ON A HANDBAG?

Hermès Birkin bags start at £4,200 for the basic model

I once thought it best not to bother putting a stop on a wife's stolen credit cards, on the basis that the thieves couldn't possibly spend money as fast as she did.

WHAT'S THE MOST USEFUL LESSON LIFE HAS TAUGHT YOU OVER THE YEARS?

Experience is what you get when you didn't get what you wanted.

WHY DO YOU WANT TO ANSWER ALL THESE QUESTIONS FROM PEOPLE?

I can't write. I can handle bits of simple-minded advert copy or a poster slogan, so answering questions is about all I'm good for. The interesting ones I get from the public give the synapses a workout, and I get to spout my views without having some probing journalist doing an interview and seeing what a thicko I am, and then having the bad manners to share their distaste with all their readers.

IF YOU HAD ANOTHER SHOT AT LIFE, IS THERE ANYTHING YOU WOULD CHANGE OR DO DIFFERENTLY?

The idea of attempting another life is alarming. I have been so favoured and gratified in my current life, I wouldn't care to push my luck.

IS ANIMAL TESTING NECESSARY?

Inhumane and barbaric, and how could it possibly make them taste better?

WHAT'S THE BEST CAREER ADVICE YOU EVER GAVE ANYONE?

Don't be irreplaceable; if you can't be replaced, you can't be promoted.

I ALWAYS FIND MYSELF FEELING GUILTY ABOUT SOMETHING. DO YOU SUFFER FROM FEELINGS OF GUILT?

In my case, a clear conscience is usually a symptom of my poor memory.

AS A 31 YEAR OLD LADY I HAVE NOT FOUND A SUITABLE LIFE PARTNER (ONE TO INDULGE THE 7 DEADLY SINS WITH) SINCE MY EARLY 20S. I AM ALLERGIC TO INTERNET DATING, A WORKAHOLIC AND NEED A MINIMUM OF 8 HOURS SLEEP EACH NIGHT. I WOULD HOWEVER LIKE TO FIND A VIRILE PARTNER. WHAT DO YOU SUGGEST? EVEN BETTER – DO YOU KNOW ANYONE?

I don't know anyone who would make a suitable life partner to someone who wants a minimum 8 hours sleep each night, and is a workaholic. His virility would appear to be a bit beside the point, under the circumstances.

WE PURCHASED TWO OILS AND FOUR LITHOGRAPHS FROM OUR NEXT DOOR NEIGHBOUR, BRUNON KOZLOWSKI, WHILST LIVING IN OMAN. NOW WE ARE LIVING BACK IN THE UK WE ARE CONSIDERING SELLING THESE PIECES. BRIEFLY, BRUNON WAS BORN IN POLAND AND STUDIED IN ITALY AT ONE TIME UNDER PICASSO. HE SCULPTS LIFE-SIZE STATUES AS WELL AS CONCENTRATING ON ART. HE IS NOW BASED IN AUSTRALIA, NEAR ADELAIDE.

HOW WOULD WE GO ABOUT GETTING A VALUATION, THEN POSSIBLY SELLING THEM? WE HAVE LOOKED ON THE NET AT VARIOUS ART WEBSITES BUT IT IS ALL QUITE BAFFLING.

 looked up Mr Kozlowski, as I am unfamiliar with his work. He is something of a polymath – a painter, sculptor, printmaker, graphic artist and teacher. Highly regarded in Australia, his work is included in the collection of The National Gallery in Canberra. I would offer your works to one of the leading auction houses in Sydney, (Shapiro Auctioneers, or Bay East Auctions), or in Melbourne (Sotheby's). Email them photos of your works and ask for estimates, and whether they will cover the transport if you consign. Good luck.

HAVE YOU EVER STOLEN, EVEN AS A CHILD?

Do you know any children who didn't shoplift sweets from Woolworths? I assumed it was an accepted rite of passage for all 6–9 year olds, and that kindly old Woolworths factored this in as a cost of doing business.

Of course, this generosity of spirit towards midget thieves like us could have been the root of Woolworths financial downfall. But I enjoyed hearing that in 1985 a pregnant woman was falsely accused of stealing a basketball by eagle-eyed store detectives.

WAS IT VANITY OVERCOMING YOUR GLUTTONY THAT MADE YOU LOSE ALL YOUR FAT ON YOUR NINE-EGGS-A-DAY-FOR-9 MONTHS DIET?

Yes. And discomfort. Without going into too many grisly details, one drawback I can chronicle about having large wobbly thighs, is a painful chafing around the testicular sac.

A particularly unpleasant memory still haunts me. I was in Bangkok airport on an especially blazing and humid day; the airport is large and requires much traversing.

My upper thighs and scrotum were being chafed unmercifully, and I was desperate to find a pharmacy to locate some talcum powder to ease my distress. No Boots, or any other chemist in sight. All I could find was a ladies' beauty product salon, and all they had available that approximated to Johnson's Baby Powder was an Estée Lauder Talc, only available in a bumper-size Christmas gift container, and at an extraordinary price. My desperation was such, I handed over my remaining Baht gratefully and poured it down into my underpants. Bliss!

As I now manfully strode away towards the boarding gate I was quickly surrounded by armed police and sniffer dogs, attracted to the trail of white powder I was depositing with every step. Two Deadly Sins punished at a stroke, in an unsparing public humiliation.

Bangkok Airport,
scene of my downfall

I'VE NEVER UNDERSTOOD "A STITCH IN TIME SAVES NINE." DO YOU?

omething about not dropping a loop when you are knitting, creating extra work. (No, just checked and it does, in fact, mean doing a stitch at the start of a tear, so the tear doesn't grow and need more stitches.) I prefer

"A drowning man is not troubled by rain."
Satisfyingly easy to comprehend

~

"A forest is an acorn."
A sentimental, but optimistic notion

~

"A new broom sweeps clean, but an old brush knows all the corners."
A favourite with pensioners, like me

~

"One of these days is none of these days."
A bit naggy, but a fair point

YOU ANSWER ME ALTHOUGH I NEVER ASK A QUESTION. WHAT AM I?
A telephone, duh. What are you, 12?

WHY DO ALMOST HALF OF ALL MARRIAGES FAIL?
Men marry women with the hope they will never change. Women marry men with the hope they will change.

TIE OR OPEN-NECKED SHIRT? WHO IS YOUR TAILOR? WHEN DO YOU SWITCH OFF YOUR BLACKBERRY?
Neither. Selfridges. No Blackberry.

WHAT IS THE BEST BOOK EVER WRITTEN?
The Bible, and My Name Is Charles Saatchi And I Am An Artoholic.

WHAT IS THE MOST MEMORABLE ADVERTISING POSTER YOU HAVE SEEN, THAT YOU WISH YOU HAD DONE?

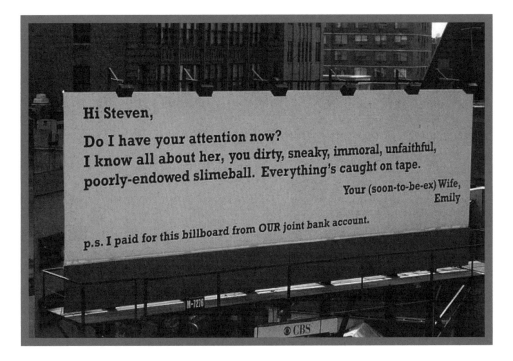

I VERY MUCH WANT TO MAKE A CAREER IN JOURNALISM, AND WITH YOUR EXPERIENCE IN THE MEDIA WORLD, WANTED TO KNOW WHAT QUALITIES YOU THINK ARE IMPORTANT TO SUCCEED IN THE NEWSPAPER PROFESSION?
A highly developed sense of rumour.

HOW DOES IT FEEL GETTING OLD?
It takes me longer to rest these days than it does to get tired. Thank you for your concern.

YOU OBVIOUSLY LIKE BROWSING ROUND MUSEUMS. DOES IT GIVE YOU SPIRITUAL PLEASURE OR AESTHETIC INSPIRATION?
I always feel sorry for the paintings, who probably hear more harebrained, batty, nonsensical remarks than anything else on earth.

DO YOU HAVE MUCH TIME FOR POLITICIANS THESE DAYS? HOW DIFFERENT ARE THEY TO MRS. THATCHER?
They always try to avoid giving offence by sitting on it.

DO YOU AGREE THAT HOLLYWOOD LEAD-ING MEN USED TO BE MORE GLAMOROUS AND EXCITING THAN THE CROP OF MORE RECENT STARS?

You're showing your age, I'm afraid, rather like me. Of course the screen heroes of Hollywood's golden age were more fabulous in every way than the male stars of today.

† Gregory Peck
† James Stewart
† Cary Grant (I)
† Gary Cooper
† William Holden
† Kirk Douglas (II)
† Montgomery Clift (III)
† Glenn Ford
† James Dean (IV)
† Marlon Brando (V)
† David Niven
† Ronald Colman
† Edward G. Robinson
† Clark Gable
† Richard Burton (VI)
† Burt Lancaster (VII)
† Humphrey Bogart
† Steve McQueen
† Lee Marvin
† Fred Astaire

† Laurence Olivier
† Spencer Tracy
† Alec Guinness
† Robert Mitchum (VIII)
† James Mason (IX)
† Charles Laughton
† Rock Hudson
† Paul Newman (X)
† Rod Steiger
† Claude Rains
† Tony Curtis
† Rex Harrison
† Sydney Poitier
† Danny Kaye
† Warren Beatty
† George C Scott
† Robert Redford (XI)
† Clint Eastwood (XII)
† John Wayne
† Jack Nicholson

I

II

III

IV

V

VI

VII

VIII

IX

X

XI

XII

NOTE

Burt Lancaster will always hold a cardinal position in my heart because he starred in the first film I remember seeing, on a memorable excursion to the Odeon Leicester Square when I was 9. He was magnificent as the *The Crimson Pirate*, and equally so in *From Here to Eternity*, *Gunfight at the O.K. Corral*, *Sweet Smell of Success*, *Run Silent Run Deep*, *Separate Tables*, *Elmer Gantry*, *Judgment at Nuremberg*, *Birdman of Alcatraz*, *Seven Days in May*, *The Train*, *The Swimmer*, *Atlantic City*, *Ulzana's Raid*. What a man (although he did have a disconcertingly fey walk).

The next generation also yielded authentic leading men.

†

† Harrison Ford (I)
† Tom Hanks (II)
† Jeff Bridges
† Tom Cruise (III)
† Bruce Willis
† Morgan Freeman (IV)
† Billy Crystal
† Robert De Niro (V)
† John Voight
† Michael Douglas (VI)
† Anthony Hopkins
† Christopher Walken (VII)
† Steve Martin (VIII)
† Harvey Keitel
† Gary Oldman
† Denzel Washington (IX)
† Dustin Hoffman
† John Travolta
† Dennis Quaid

† Michael Caine (X)
† George Clooney (XI)
† William Hurt
† Mickey Rourke
† Tommy Lee Jones (XII)
† Gene Hackman (XIII)
† Sean Connery
† Robert Duvall (XIV)
† Bill Murray
† Jim Carrey
† John Candy
† Michael Keaton
† Al Pacino
† Robert Shaw
† Richard Dreyfuss
† Albert Finney (XV)
† Liam Neeson
† Ryan O'Neal
† Richard Gere (XVI)

I

II

III

IV

V

VI

VII

VIII

IX

X

XI

XII

XIII

XIV

XV

XVI

Of the current big names, very few of real note.

† Matt Damon
† Will Smith
† Vince Vaughn
† Daniel Craig
† Josh Brolin
† Russell Crowe (I)
† Leonardo DiCaprio (II)

† Viggo Mortensen
† Daniel Day-Lewis (III)
† Liev Schreiber
† Timothy Olyphant
† Ryan Gosling
† Johnny Depp (IV)
† Philip Seymour Hoffman

I

II

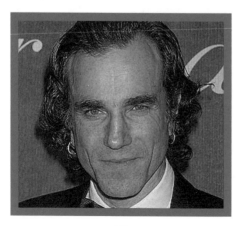

III

IV

Sadly, I find it best to avoid any films starring many of today's heroes, who are so wooden they would stiffen any script into rigor mortis, or are simply too hammy to digest.

† Adam Sandler
† Orlando Bloom
† Jim Caviezel
† David Duchovny
† Tim Roth
† Billy Bob Thornton
† Don Cheadle
† Antonio Banderas
† Keanu Reeves
† Jared Leto
† Adrian Brody
† Ewan McGregor
† Ben Affleck
† Ashton Kutcher
† Josh Hartnett
† Paul Walker
† Rob Schneider

† Shia LaBeouf
† Freddie Prinze Jr.
† Elijah Wood
† Matthew Broderick
† Will Ferrell
† Mike Myers
† Clive Owen
† Sam Rockwell
† Joseph Fiennes
† Christian Slater
† Mark Ruffalo
† Tobey Maguire
† Ben Kingsley
† Andy Garcia
† Stephen Dorff
† Cuba Gooding Jr.
† Tim Allen

† Vin Diesel
† Jason Statham
† Hayden Christensen
† Wesley Snipes
† Matthew McConaughey
† Patrick Dempsey
† Martin Lawrence
† Timothy Dalton
† Dougray Scott
† Sean Bean
† Jake Gyllenhaal
† Matthew Perry
† Chris Rock
† Paul Rudd
† Forest Whitaker
† Robert Downey Jr.
† Robert Carlyle

I defy anyone sentient to sit through more than 20 minutes of any of his movies

AS A SOON-TO-BE 65 YEAR OLD FINE ART GRADUATE HOW CAN I MAKE ANY KIND OF MARK ON THE CONTEMPORARY ART WORLD?

Carmen Herrera at 94, who now has a work in
the collection of the Museum of Modern Art, New York

I hope you find Carmen Herrera, who sold her first painting when she was 89, as inspiring as I do: "Perhaps it's been a good thing I was able to work for so many years without recognition. I was left alone to refine and distil my art for decades, paring things down to their essence. I have no regrets, no complaints, and my work is more important to me than ever. I'm not as well as I would like to be, but as soon as I begin painting all my aches and pains disappear.

I don't know how I would have reacted if I had been more successful when I was young. Now it's nice, and I have more money than I could ever have imagined earlier in my life. Yet I'm not overwhelmed by it at all. I've always been a private person, and my work is my private life – I'd resent it if I felt people were intruding when I was trying to paint. But it is very pleasant to be recognized a little bit – I've made it on to the cover of *The New York Times* without having to kill anyone. All I had to do was get old. The world came to me, eventually. I just had to wait 94 years, that's all."

Carmen Herrera, Shocking Pink No.20, 1949

IF YOU HAD AN ALCOHOLIC SPOUSE, WHOM YOU LOVED, BUT WHO WAS STEADFASTLY WRECKING THEIR OWN HAPPINESS, OUR CHILDREN'S HAPPINESS, THEIR HEALTH AND INDEED MY HAPPINESS – WHILST ALSO AT THE SAME TIME MAINTAINING THAT CHANGES WOULD BE EFFECTED, AND HELP SOUGHT – HAVING MADE THIS STATEMENT FOR THE PAST 3/4 YEARS AND NONE OF IT HAPPENING – TELL ME WHAT WOULD YOU DO. YOU SHOULD ALSO FACTOR INTO YOUR AN-SWER THAT WE HAVE NO MONEY, ALL OUR MONEY BEING TIED UP INTO OUR HOUSE... WHICH WE ARE CURRENTLY TAKING TO THE MARKET, THAT I AM 50 AND THE LAST TIME I WORKED WAS 8 YEARS AGO AS HEAD OF A DESIGN AGENCY... SO NOT FIT FOR ANY PURPOSE... AND WE HAVE TWO CHIL-DREN IN THEIR EARLY TEENS. BASICALLY DO I STAY OR DO I GO?

 know a number of ex-alcoholics, and they all say the same thing. You can only give up when you hit rock bottom, and have to claw your way out if you can, with all the help you can get.
My advice is to give your husband a taste of rock bottom. Move out with your children, and stay with friends or family for a month. Hopefully that will inspire him to face the depths he has reached, and get him into an AA programme

with a total commitment to win his battle. You are better off, for you and your children's sake, to stay away and have faith in your own resourcefulness. You are only 50, and shouldn't give up on the skills you built heading a design agency. You are certainly as fit for purpose as I am. More professional advice would insist that you ask your spouse to leave, and have him stay with friends and family, until he gets a grip. Why should you give up living in your house until you have sold it? Either route will work, or will not, but at the very least your life can be moving forward in the meantime.

I'M A VERY SQUEAMISH PERSON AND I ONCE SAW A MAT COLLISHAW PIECE AT YOUR GALLERY WITH A BULLET HOLE IN SOMEONE'S HEAD – I NEARLY THREW UP ON THE SPOT. WHAT MAKES YOU QUEASY?

I have a shaving mirror that shows the face in great detail.

WHAT'S YOUR MOST USUAL WAKING THOUGHT IN THE MORNING?

Start the day off with a smile and get it over with.

WHAT MAKES YOU THINK YOU HAVE THE RIGHT TO PONTIFICATE TO OTHER PEOPLE?

Why do they call it common sense, when it is so rare?

HOW REGULARLY DO YOU FIND YOURSELF DEPRESSED, AND WHAT DO YOU DO ABOUT IT?

Nothing. Depression is merely anger without enthusiasm.

THE CHILDREN LIVING NEXT DOOR ARE BEING HORRIBLY ABUSED BY THEIR PARENTS. THE ONLY WAY TO STOP THE ABUSE IS TO ADOPT THE CHILDREN AND CARE FOR THEM IN YOUR HOME. WOULD YOU?

The alternative is to give our children to the parents next door to you, who are probably far better at discipline than we are, helping create strong, if slightly damaged, adults.

WHAT IS THE BEST ROCK ALBUM EVER?
Now That's What I Call Music 1. It must have been
magnificent, because they have now reached
Now That's What I Call Music 79.

NOTE
Here are the tracks from *Now That's What I Call Music 1*,
a couple of which are not entirely terrible.

† Phil Collins, *You Can't Hurry Love*
† Duran Duran, *Is There Something*
† UB40, *Red Red Wine*
† Heaven 17, *Temptation* (I)
† Tina Turner, *Let's Stay Together*
† The Human League, *(Keep Feeling) Fascination* (II)
† Kajagoogoo, *Big Apple* (III)
† KC and the Sunshine Band, *Give It Up* (IV)
† Malcolm McLaren, *Double Dutch*
† Limahl, *Only For Love* (V)
† Men Without Hats, *Safety Dance* (VI)
† Kajagoogoo, *Too Shy*
† Mike Oldfield, *Moonlight Shadow*
† Men at Work, *Down Under*
† Rock Steady Crew, *(Hey You) The Rock Steady Crew*
† Paul Young, *Wherever I Lay My Hat (That's My Home)* (VII)
† Peabo Bryson & Roberta Flack, *Tonight I Celebrate My Love*
† New Edition *Candy Girl*
† UB40, *Please Don't Make Me Cry*
† Howard Jones, *New Song*
† Tracey Ullman, *They Don't Know*
† Bonnie Tyler, *Total Eclipse of the Heart* (VIII)
† Will Powers, *Kissing with Confidence*
† Genesis, *That's All*
† The Cure, *The Lovecats*
† Simple Minds, *Waterfront*
† Culture Club, *Karma Chameleon* (IX)
† Rod Stewart, *Baby Jane* (X)
† Madness, *The Sun and the Rain* (XI)
† Culture Club, *Victims*

I

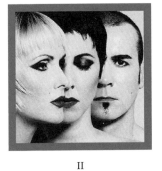

II

III

IV

V

VI

VII

VIII

IX

X

XI

XII

A rarely enjoyed rear view of *Venus de Milo*, mum of Eros, carved by Alexander of Antioch between 130 and 100 BC

On an encouraging note, in 1820 a Greek peasant on the island of Milos was digging in his field and unearthed several carved blocks of stone. As he burrowed deeper he found four statues – three figures of Hermes and one of Aphrodite, goddess of love. Three weeks later an archaeological expedition arrived by ship, purchased the Aphrodite and took it to France. Louis XVIII gave it the name *Venus De Milo* and presented it to the Louvre, where it became one of the most famous works of art in history.

More recently a couple in a suburb of Milwaukee, Wisconsin, asked an art appraiser to look at a painting in their home. While he was there, he examined another picture that the couple had thought was a reproduction of a work by Van Gogh. It turned out to be an 1886 original. On March 10, 1991 the painting *Still Life With Flowers* sold at auction for $1.4 million.

WHAT IS THE BEST PLACE (GENERAL OR SPECIFIC) TO SELL A LARGE METAL SCULPTURE WHICH WE RESCUED FROM GOING TO THE SCRAP MAN?

Unless it's by Alberto Giacometti, Henry Moore, Anthony Caro or a few other proper metalworkers, it's best to give it back to the scrap man. You could try a car-boot sale if it will fit in your boot, or if you feel particularly blessed, photograph it and show it to a Sotheby's expert, just in case it's a long-lost Brancusi worth £5 million.

WHAT'S YOUR FAVOURITE JOKE?

All those who believe in telekinesis, raise my hand.

HAVE YOU EVER PRAISED AN EMPLOYEE AND NOT MEANT IT?

I praise myself all the time, and am most sincere about it.

WHAT IS THE GREATEST MYSTERY OF THE UNIVERSE?

Why, if ignorance is bliss, there aren't more happy people in the world.

AFTER MARTYRING MYSELF IN KITCHENS, WORKING LIKE A SLAVE FOR OTHERS, I GOT THE GUTS AND THE COURAGE TO BREAK FREE FROM MY MEDIOCRE EXISTENCE AND SET UP WWW.SPATULACATERING.CO.UK WHICH IS TEN MONTHS OLD THIS MONTH. I BUILT IT ON A WING, A PRAYER AND A SHOESTRING, WITHOUT GIVING UP MY FREEDOM AND REVERTING BACK TO COOK-ING IN SOME FACILE & FUTILE RESTAURANT. HOW DO I MARKET "SPATULA CATERING" WITHOUT SPENDING A FORTUNE ON THE USUAL & UNCREATIVE OPTIONS THAT FAIL TO GENERATE BUSINESS?

ou have a nice website and have attracted some impressive clients for your catering services. Sadly, the business you are pursuing is a notoriously tricky one, with grindingly small margins and a barrage of fiddly problems. Instead of cooking in someone else's facile and futile restaurant, why not open your own fecund and fertile establishment, which could prove more satisfying and profitable with your set of skills.

It's easier to attract a roomful of customers to a good local restaurant, where word-of-mouth can take care of promotion, than to constantly seek new clients for a catering business. But of course, you could still look for catering gigs on the side; and if you were to enter BBC Masterchef, and win...

I was easily bored from a young age

ARE YOU EASILY BORED?

arcolepsically. As we all know, a bore is a man who has nothing to say and says it anyway. Rather like my answers to these questions you might feel. Here are my favourite students of boredom.

†

The man who suspects his own tediousness
is yet to be born.
THOMAS B. ALDRICH

I am quite serious when I say that I do not
believe there are, on the whole earth besides, so many
intensified bores as in these United States. No
man can form an adequate idea of the real meaning
of the word, without coming here.
CHARLES DICKENS

I spent a year in that town, one Sunday.
WARWICK DEEPING

His shortcoming is his long staying.
LEWIS L. LEWISOHN

The nice thing about being a celebrity is that if
you bore people, they think it's their fault.
HENRY KISSINGER

†

CAN YOU PLEASE EXPLAIN THE PSYCHOL-
OGY BEHIND SOME APPARENTLY CRAZY ADS,
WHICH HAVE BAFFLED ME AND MANY OTH-
ERS, FOR YEARS? THE PRIME EXAMPLE: A TV
AD OF AN AUDI CAR RACING ALONG A BEACH
THROUGH HUNDREDS OF RED CRABS! THAT
AD WAS DEVISED BY EXPERTS AND WILL
HAVE COST A FORTUNE, SO IT MUST HAVE
SOLD A LOT OF CARS. BUT HOW AND WHY?
AND HOW WILL THIS HAVE WORKED BETTER
THAN SIMPLE DETAILS OF PERFORMANCE
AND RELIABILITY ETC? ALSO, CAN YOU
RECOMMEND A BOOK WHICH EXPLAINS
THE PSYCHOLOGY BEHIND
SUCH ADS.

on't scratch your head pondering how to
analyze commercials like these. I assure you
no sentient intelligence was involved in any
process of producing the advertisement.
Neither the manufacturer nor the advertising
agent had even the mollusc of an idea about how to promote their car, so they hired a hack director to come up
with a striking visual mnemonic, striking only in its irrel-
evance and dimwittedness (car with crabs on beach). I
would be most surprised if it sold any cars whatsoever.
That's the nice thing about the advertising business;
it provides gainful employment for
people like me, who are a
bit on the dense
side.

I READ THAT THE PRADO MUSEUM IN MADRID IS YOUR FAVOURITE. CAN YOU NAME THE OTHER MUSEUMS THAT HAVE INSPIRED YOU?

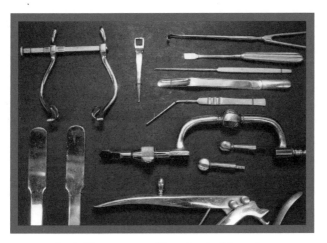

Surgical instruments used in performing lobotomies,
the medication of choice from the 1930s to the late 1950s.

All the obvious ones, I'm afraid. But I have four less celebrated establishments that are worthy of attention.

I

The Glore Psychiatric Museum in St Joseph, Missouri, USA. Brings to life the history of psychiatric treatment through dioramas, models, reproductions, from the early uses of a sharp stick or club, the Middle Age treatments of dunking, blistering, or the ever popular bleeding. By the 20th century psychiatric treatment had evolved to include icy baths, tranquillizers and electro shock therapy.

II

Kansas Barbed Wire Museum in Lacrosse, USA. Exhibits over 2000 barbed wire varieties with examples manufactured in the glory years between 1870 and 1890, included in its Barbed Wire Hall of Fame.

III

The Icelandic Phallological Museum in Husavic. Contains a collection of over 100 penises belonging to almost all the land and sea mammals that can be found in Iceland. Visitors to the museum will encounter 30 specimens belonging to 12 different kinds of whale, one specimen from a polar bear, and eighteen originating from various species of seal and walrus.

IV

The Sulabh Museum of Toilets in New Delhi, India. Visitors can follow the evolution of the lavatory in various cultures around the world.

Charles Darwin, author of
On the Origin of Species

James Joyce, author of impenetrable books

IF YOU COULD ASK ANY QUESTION TO CHARLES DARWIN, JAMES JOYCE, JESUS CHRIST, ADOLF HITLER, HENRY VIII, MARILYN MONROE, MOSES, WHAT WOULD IT BE?

†

CHARLES DARWIN	How was your theory of evolution received when you arrived at the Pearly Gates?
JAMES JOYCE	Have you ever tried reading one of your books?
JESUS CHRIST	What does your middle initial 'H' stand for?
ADOLF HITLER	Would it have all been different if you had found success with your paintings?
HENRY VIII	Which is more painful, gout or syphilis?
MARILYN MONROE	Is it worth dying young to become an eternal icon?
MOSES	How did you like Charlton Heston in *The Ten Commandments*?

WHAT ARE YOU READING?
Your question.

WHAT IS THE WORST INSULT ANYONE HAS PAID YOU?
You are no longer beneath my contempt.

DO YOU HAVE A PARTY TRICK?
Not attending.

WHAT IS YOUR GREATEST WEAKNESS?
Indisiciv... Indesiss... Indesiciv... Indecisiveness.

WHAT DO YOU THINK OF THE TATE'S TURNER PRIZE?
As the old saying goes, all anybody needs to know about prizes is that Mozart never won one.

WHAT IS YOUR GREATEST AIM IN LIFE?

would like to ride the world's Five Fastest Roller Coasters. Possibly this ambition is to remain unfulfilled, seeing as how I grow weak-kneed just looking at the chilling rides at the local fun fair, and am regularly stretchered away foaming with terror and vomit after watching my foolish children whirl around, giggling deliriously in one of those wonky looking contraptions.

As a craven jellyfish throughout my life, I would welcome leaving my offspring something to revere, something rugged and admirable. I intend to be handcuffed into the following rides and will demonstrate my resolution and mettle.

I

Kingda Ka (128 mph) Not just the fastest, but also the tallest roller coaster in the world. A hydraulic launch mechanism rockets the train from 0 to 128 mph in 3.5 seconds, twisting 90 degrees to a height of 456 feet, then descends straight down through a 270-degree spiral.

II

Top Thrill Dragster (120 mph) 420 feet tall, the ride has a 90 degree counter-clockwise descent, where passengers experience 1.67 g forces.

III

Dodonpa (107 mph) Has a compressed air launch that takes it to 107mph in less than two seconds, ascending a sweeping overbanked curve, with extreme negative g forces.

IV

Tower of Terror (100 mph) Electromagnetically powered, it climbs to 38 storeys high followed by a 6.5 second free-fall and a reverse 90 degree turn.

V

Steel Dragon (95 mph) Has the largest track length of 8133 ft, and is the world tallest complete-circuit coaster.

Kingda Ka – Six Flags Great Adventure, Jackson Township, New Jersey, USA

Dodonpa – Fuji-Q Highland, Fujiyoshida, Yamanashi, Japan

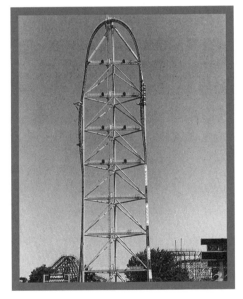

Top Thrill Dragster – Cedar Point, Sandusky, Ohio, USA

Tower of Terror – Dreamworld, Coomera, Queensland, Australia

Steel Dragon 2000 – Nagashima Spa Land, Mie Prefecture, Japan

WHAT IS YOUR MOST HATED BUSINESS EXPRESSION?

 will give 110%, step up to the plate, hit the ground running, deliver pro-active solutions, and blue-sky thinking, 24/7, in a worst-case scenario.

WHEN OUT TO DINNER WITH MY BOSS I TEND TO GET BORED VERY QUICKLY. THESE INVITATIONS ARE COMPULSORY ATTENDANCE. MY QUESTION IS THIS: AS THE MEAL WEARS ON IS IT BETTER FOR HIM TO CATCH ME REGULARLY CHECKING THE TIME BY LOOKING AT HIS WATCH, OR MY OWN?

 f you are guileless enough to be spotted doing either, you deserve very many boring dinners with your boss.
One of the purposes of business entertaining is to be entertaining; as the employee in the gathering this burden rests upon you.

DID YOU EVER THINK YOU'D END UP WHERE YOU ARE?

I always wanted to be Pope, and haven't given up yet.

WHAT WAS THE BEST PIECE OF ADVICE YOUR FATHER GAVE YOU?

Always remember you are unique and just like everyone else.

WHICH QUOTATION BY A FAMOUS HISTORICAL FIGURE DO YOU MOST ADMIRE?

Steve Martin: "You know 'the look' women get when they want to have sex? Me neither."

I'M BY CHOICE A FAIRLY LAZY PERSON, AND FIND PEOPLE LIKE YOU, ALWAYS APPARENTLY THRASHING AROUND IN A HYPERACTIVE WAY, CHASING THEIR TAIL, RATHER PATHETIC. WHAT'S WRONG WITH A MORE RELAXED APPROACH TO LIFE?

 'm flattered you consider me even a little bit active, as I assure you I am far more idle than you could possibly be. My favourite politician was asked "Mr. Churchill, sir, to what do you attribute your success in life?" Without time for pause or hesitation, he replied "Conservation of energy. Never stand up when you can sit down, and never sit down when you can lie down." He then got into a chauffeured limousine.

WHEN WAS THE LAST TIME YOU LOST YOUR TEMPER AT WORK?

 just screeched at myself for some stupidity or other, and would have headbutted me into a heap, if it were possible.

CAN YOU TELL ME WHAT IS YOUR FAVOURITE PAINTING?

Piero della Francesca. *Polyptych of the Misericordia*. 1444–64. Mixed technique on panel. 273 × 330 cm. Pinacoteca Comunale, Sansepolcro, Italy.

oo many favourites, hundreds in fact, but this Piero is the one that popped to the head of the queue when I read your question. In half an hour, it could be a pet Velazquez, or a Goya, or some new, young artist from Croydon. If you have never been to see the Piero della Francesca museum in Sansepolcro, Italy, drop everything and get the next flight.

YOU SEEM QUITE DISMISSIVE OF MOST ART EXPERTS, ART CURATORS AND ART CRITICS. IS THIS JUST BASED ON ARROGANCE, OR EXPERIENCE?

or 47 days in 1961, Matisse's *Le Bateau* was hanging upside down in the Museum of Modern Art, New York. Apparently none of the 34 of the Museum's curatorial staff, nor 280 art critics, noticed. The mistake was spotted by a member of the public, Genevieve Hubert, a stockbroker.

At least MoMA didn't hang their Matisse *The Red Studio* upside down, one of the most beautiful paintings in the world.

DO YOU BELIEVE IN COUNTING YOUR BLESSINGS?

It depends what you define as blessings.

Is it a blessing to be right-handed, because 2500 left-handed people are killed each year using products for right-handed people?

~

Is it a blessing not to have been hit by lightning, regularly, as lightning strikes about 6000 times every minute around the world?

~

Is it a blessing not to be a poet looking for a rhyme for orange, or purple, or month, because no words in the dictionary can do it?

~

Is it a blessing not to be an earthworm, because baby robins each eat 14 feet of earth worms every day?

My point is that counting your blessings is a flawed concept, only of sustenance to those needing to bolster themselves with feelings of gratitude that everything isn't much, much worse. I subscribe to the 'Life is a Roller Coaster / Just Gotta Ride It' doctrine of existence. Embrace its ups and downs equally – both the heady pleasures and the despairing anguish. They make the day more enthralling.

YOU STRIKE ME AS A BIT OF A KNOW-ALL. WHAT MAKES YOU THINK OF YOURSELF AS AN EXPERT ON EVERY-THING?

I know that chewing gum while peeling onions will stop you from crying.

~

I know that right-handed people chew food on the right side of their mouths, and left-handed people on the left.

~

I know that dalmatians are born without spots.

~

I know that when you blush, the lining of your stomach also turns red.

~

I know that the lion who roars in the MGM logo is named Volney.

~

I know it cost $7 million to build the *Titanic*, and $200 million to make a film about it.

~

I know that the little plastic things on the end of shoelaces are called aglets.

~

I know that only rabbits and parrots can see behind themselves without turning their heads.

~

I know that when hippos are upset their sweat turns red.

~

I know that most football players run 7 miles in the course of a game.

~

I know that the three wise monkeys are called mizaru (see no evil)

kikazaru (hear no evil) and iwazaru (speak no evil).

~

I know that bats always turn left when exiting a cave.

~

I know that every time you sneeze some of your brain cells die.

~

I know that women blink nearly twice as often as men.

~

I know that the colour blue has a relaxing effect, causing the brain to release calming hormones.

~

I know Colgate faced problems in Spain marketing their toothpaste, because Colgate in Spanish translates into 'go hang yourself'.

~

I know the names of Popeye's four nephews are Pipeye, Peepeye, Pupeye and Poopeye.

~

I know a lightning bolt generates temperatures five times hotter than those found at the sun's surface.

~

I know that almost half of the newspapers in the world are published in the United States and Canada.

~

I know that the most popular first name in the world is Muhammad.

~

I know most lipstick contains fish scales.

~

I know that no piece of square dry paper can be folded in half more than seven times.

I know that a group of geese on the ground is a gaggle, a group of geese in the air is a skein.

~

I know that the world's termites outweigh the world's humans ten to one.

~

I know the cockroach can live several weeks with its head cut off, finally dying from starvation.

~

I know that you are born with 300 bones, but when you get to be an adult you only have 206.

~

I know that in ancient Egypt you would have probably died by the time you were 30.

~

I know that more people use blue toothbrushes than red ones.

~

I know that like fingerprints, everyone's tongue print is different.

~

I know that the giraffe can clean its ears with its 21 inch tongue.

~

I know that the colours red, yellow and orange are used in fast food restaurants because they are colours that stimulate hunger.

~

I know that the dot that appears over the letter 'i' is called a tittle.

~

I know that the phrase 'always a bridesmaid, never a bride' originates from an advertisement for Listerine mouthwash from 1924.

I know that Malcolm X's real name is Malcolm Little.

~

I know that deer sleep for five minutes a day.

~

I know that Donald Duck comics were banned in Finland because he doesn't wear pants.

~

I know that Ringo Starr appeared in an advertisement for apple sauce in Japan. His name means 'apple sauce' in Japanese.

Far from being a know-all, as you can see I have accumulated lots of utterly irrelevant scraps of information that are no use to me, or anyone else. Sadly, I am not enough of a know-all to know how to delete this rubbish clogging my memory banks, leaving me quite unable to recall any piece of information that I actually want to retrieve.

WHAT DO YOU THINK ABOUT IQ? IS IT HUMAN FICTION, OR IS IT REALLY TELLING US SOMETHING ABOUT OURSELVES?

 veryone knows that IQ tests only tell you how good you are at doing IQ tests. I remember having an implausibly high IQ when I was tested in my youth, and I'm pretty certain I was even thicker then.

I HAVE SENT YOU THIS RORSCHACH
INKBLOT IMAGE. I AM A CLINICAL PSYCHOL-
OGIST AND WOULD BE VERY INTERESTED
TO LEARN WHAT COMES TO YOUR MIND
WHEN YOU LOOK AT THIS?

I see a lush yellow cornfield with a lazy stream coursing
through it. There is a scarecrow with a straw hat in the
middle of the field and a grey mare eating grass on the
banks of the stream, being watched by a white swan. Two
young children are playing with hula hoops at the corner
of the field, underneath a sycamore tree, shading them
from the bright sunlight.

A fisherman is sitting on the bank opposite the horse with
his dog, a collie, panting at his side. An air balloon is glid-
ing in the sky above with a group of five people being
carried in its basket.

An ice cream van can be seen on the small road at the end of
the field next to the farmhouse. Smoke is curling out of the
chimney in the farmhouse, and the farmer's wife is carrying
a tray of tea and biscuits to her farmer husband working
in the yard outside, shepherding his sheep into their barn.

A windmill turns idly next to the farmhouse.

A young couple are sunbathing on top of a large haystack
next to the sycamore tree.

Five nuns are having a picnic beneath a willow tree, point-
ing at a flock of thrushes flying above.

A small herd of black cows is grazing on the grassy hill
beyond the farm, being tended by a farm worker in dun-
garees, smoking a pipe. Do you see
the same?

WERE YOU FRIENDS WITH ANDY WARHOL? WHAT CAN YOU TELL ME ABOUT HIM THAT PEOPLE DON'T KNOW?

went to Warhol's studio when his career was at a low ebb. He had achieved great attention in the Pop era, but by the late-Seventies he was considered rather undignified by the art world, because he would paint commissioned portraits of rich people or celebrities.

Nobody much was particularly interested in his work at the time; he was thought to be simply re-working his greatest hits, making multiple versions of his signature paintings in a bulging colour swatch of variants.

From underneath his bed, Warhol pulled out a rolled canvas of *100 Marilyns,* 18ft long, which he had made in 1962. He considered it his masterpiece, and he was saving it for a rainy day. It must have been very rainy the day I visited, because he offered me the picture, for what at the time seemed an insanely high price, but one that I was most grateful to accept. It became the centerpiece of the Warhol exhibition that opened my first gallery in Boundary Road, London in 1985.

I found him completely engaging, and learnt that he kept a box next to his working table where he deposited anything that interested him – photos, newspapers clippings, magazine articles, letters, and any ephemera that had captured his limited attention span. At the end of each month, the box was sealed, the date added, a new box started.

There are over 600 boxes that have been archived, contents varying from a mummified foot, Caroline Kennedy's birthday cake, a 17th century book on wrestling, drawings of Hollywood icons, sketches of Jean Harlow's dress, studies of Clark Gable's boots.

He was a committed shopper, and daily added to his ever-growing collection of biscuit tins, native American folk art, taxidermy specimens, exotic jewellery, perfume bottles, autographed pictures of movie stars, World's Fair souvenirs, cowboy boots, art deco furniture, dental moulds and his trademark collection of white wigs. Warhol believed department stores and thrift shops were just another form of museum. He provided me with one of the more interesting days in my life.

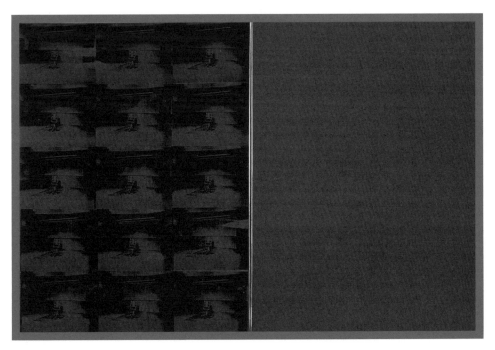

My personal favourite of the breathtaking (even if I say so myself, and I do, regularly) selection of Warhol in our first exhibition at the Boundary Road gallery: *Blue Electric Chair*, 1963, immense in scale, spellbinding in presence – alongside *100 Marilyns*, one of the masterpieces of the 20th century.

NOTHING IN ART MOVES ME AS MUCH AS THE BEAUTY OF NATURE. I DON'T SUPPOSE YOU AGREE?

I certainly do.

YOU SEEM TO REPRESENT ALL I FIND UN-PLEASANT ABOUT THE MODERN WORLD. PEOPLE LIKE ME, WHO DON'T COURT PERSONAL VALIDATION, BELIEVE IN PUTTING OTHER PEOPLE FIRST. TODAY EVERYTHING IS ABOUT GRATIFICATION OF THE SELF, AND CHOOSING OUR OWN HAPPINESS OVER ANYONE ELSE'S. WHATEVER HAPPENED TO THE VALUES I ADHERE TO, LIKE DUTY, MORALITY, RIGHTEOUSNESS, AND THE BELIEF THAT GOODNESS IS ITS OWN REWARD?

ou may sound like a very good person, but in fact you just suffer from the disease to please. And what's more you seem to want to be congratulated for it. Apparently, goodness is not its own reward.

HOW WOULD YOUR P.A. DESCRIBE YOU?

I daren't ask, and would appreciate it if you didn't.

IF YOU WERE AN ISLAND, WHERE WOULD YOU BE? IF YOU WERE A MUSICAL NOTE, WHAT WOULD YOU BE? IF YOU WERE A PACKAGE, WHAT WOULD YOU BE?

Have you thought of seeking medical help?

DID YOU DISAPPOINT YOUR PARENTS?

It's a little late to ask them now, unfortunately.

WHAT WAS YOUR WORST BUSINESS DISASTER?

Too many to recall. You never learn anything by doing it right.

IF YOU COULD WIN A GOLD MEDAL AT THE OLYMPIC GAMES WHICH SPORT WOULD YOU WANT IT TO BE?

hat's the point? The last time gold medals were made out of real gold was in 1912. I don't believe the Zimmer Frame, which I assume I will excel at any day now, has yet to be accepted as an Olympic Sport.

YOU HAVE BEEN REGULARLY SAVAGED BY CRITICS. HOW DO YOU COPE WITH THAT?

 obody does criticism like John Simon, the illustrious New York film and theatre commentator. Here's his charming review of Elizabeth Taylor as Katherina in *The Taming Of The Shrew*:

'Just how garish her commonplace accent, squeakily shrill voice, and the childish petulance with which she delivers her lines, my pen is neither scratchy nor leaky enough to convey.'

I am obviously delighted he doesn't cover art for a British newspaper. Sometimes a horrific review can turn out to be quite helpful. The *Sensation* exhibition was so universally panned, it aroused curiosity and ended up doing well for the Royal Academy's box office receipts. And critic Eugene Field made an instant celebrity of one hapless actor with this notice:

'Last night Mr Creston Clarke played King Lear at the Tabor Grand. All through the five acts of that Shakespearean tragedy he played the King as though under momentary apprehension that someone else was about to play the Ace.'

Savage reviews are satisfying for the pundit, who gets to show off his rapier wit, and entertaining for the reader. Only the subject of the review is temporarily chastened, and rarely is a critic found garroted or battered to death by one of his enraged victims.

Elizabeth Taylor as Katherina in Franco Zeffirelli's *The Taming of the Shrew*, co-starring Richard Burton as Petruchio.

IF A CAT HAS NINE LIVES, HOW MANY LIVES HAS A DOG?

You have stumped me. But the dog here seems to be on his second, at least.

WHAT'S THE FASTEST WAY A MAN LIKE ME, LAZY AND WITH LIMITED BUSINESS SKILLS, IN A MIDDLING JOB WITH FEW PROSPECTS, CAN MAKE A LOT OF MONEY?

arry a very rich woman who is too proud to let her husband work.

Every sensible man I know has always fantasized about finding, and securing, a lovely wife who is considerate enough to be exceptionally wealthy.

The only friend who pulled off this wonder ended up with a pleasant-enough spouse, profoundly rich, but unfortunately also profoundly insecure and jealous and who didn't trust him an inch. If she didn't find strange hairs on his jacket, she simply accused him of having an affair with a bald woman. His marriage enabled him to spend each day of his pampered life indulging his desire to be swanning around posh golf clubs, but perhaps he ended up paying too high a price for membership.

DO YOU THINK ARTISTS ARE MORE INTELLIGENT THAN OTHER PEOPLE?

I have always been hesitant about visiting artists' studios, and discovering that work I have admired has been made by someone nitwitted. This can be disconcerting if you believe an artist paints with his brains, not with his hands.

DO YOU EVER COMPLAIN TO NEWSPAPER EDITORS IF AN ARTICLE IS NASTY ABOUT YOU?

Never pick a fight with someone who buys ink by the barrel.

WOULD YOU DESCRIBE YOURSELF AS A GENTLEMAN?

Certainly. On the basis that a gentleman is a man who can play the accordion but doesn't.

I MET A WOMAN WHO YOU ONCE ESCORTED FOR A WHILE, A BEAUTIFUL LADY CALLED HELENA. SHE SAID YOU WERE ONLY INTERESTED IN WORK, OR PLAYING SCRABBLE AND POKER. APPARENTLY WHEN SHE TOLD YOU TO CHOOSE BETWEEN HER OR YOUR PLAYMATES, YOU CARRIED ON REGARDLESS AND LOST HER, AS SHE THOUGHT YOU JUVENILE. RING ANY BELLS?

Another one of my near Mrs.

DID YOU HAVE AN IMAGINARY FRIEND WHEN YOU WERE A BOY?

He's still around. He hasn't aged. He is still hyper-critical of everything I do, as paranoid as ever, still controlling and dismissive and with the same self-righteous, overbearing attitude. His voice is in my head at all times, scolding my every error, ungracious and belittling about any minor success I may occasionally have. Anyway that's what I told my psychiatrist, at our only meeting, in order to make our session more interesting and memorable for him. He has since written a much-admired paper for *The Lancet* medical journal, describing my problem, where I am referred to as Patient 27. Did I mention my imaginary friend is Caligula?

Gaius Julius Caesar Augustus Germanicus (31 Aug AD 12–24 Jan AD 41), Rome's third emperor in succession to Tiberius, more commonly known by his agnomen Caligula.

WHEN I THINK OF THE MOST INSPIRING AND CHARISMATIC MEN OF GREATNESS OF THE MODERN ERA, I THINK OF MARTIN LUTHER KING, NELSON MANDELA AND WINSTON CHURCHILL. WHO DO YOU LOOK TO?
I look to the great mass murderers, the leaders who were so inspiring and charismatic, they were able to convince their own people to kill their neighbours in the millions.

MAO ZEDONG
(China, 1947–76)
Mao Zedong was the leader of the Chinese Communist Party from 1949 until his death in 1976. During Chairman Mao's reign, some 70 million Chinese, along with countless Tibetans, Mongolians, Manchus, Koreans, Hmong, Uyghurs, and other nationalities, perished under his watch.

MENGISTU HAILE MARIAM (I)
(Ethiopia, 1974–91)
During Mengistu's "Dergue" regime tens of thousands of Ethiopians were tortured, murdered or "disappeared". Many more died of starvation, under the watchful eyes of his supporters.

HIDEKI TOJO (II)
(Japan, 1941–44)
Tojo is considered responsible for the murder of more than 8 million civilians in China, Korea, the Philippines, Indochina, and in the other Pacific island nations, as well as the murder of tens of thousands of Allied POWs. His followers conducted government-sanctioned biological experiments on POWs and Chinese civilians.

JOSEPH STALIN (III)
(USSR, 1934–39)
Estimates of his victims vary between 20 and 28 million. 18 million were sent to the Gulag Archipelago work camps, never returning alive. Others were simply starved to death.

ADOLF HITLER
(Germany, 1939–1945)
The architect of a highly efficient and systematic genocide of over 6 million in the Holocaust, Hitler's leadership, and bid for territorial conquest and racial subjugation caused the deaths of millions more.

JEAN KAMBANDA
(Rwanda, 1994)
His followers were responsible for the mass killing of hundreds of thousands of Rwanda's minority Tutsis and the moderates of its Hutu majority. Most estimates are of a death toll between 800,000 and 1,000,000.

SUHARTO (IV)
(East Timor, West Papua, 1966–98)
Up to two million were killed following a coup attempt in 1965. The killings were on such a scale that the

disposal of the corpses created a severe sanitation problem in East Java and northern Sumatra. Over 250,000 deaths followed the invasion of East Timor in 1975 and thousands more were killed in various Indonesian provinces.

I   II

III   IV

IDI AMIN (V)
(Uganda, 1969–1979)

To secure his regime Amin's followers launched a campaign of persecution against rival tribes and Obote supporters, murdering between 100,000 and 500,000. Among those to die were ordinary citizens, former and serving Cabinet ministers, the chief justice, Supreme Court judges, diplomats, academics, educators, prominent Roman Catholic and Anglican clergy, senior bureaucrats, medical practitioners, bankers, tribal leaders, business executives, journalists and a large number of foreigners.

V   VI

POL POT (VI)
(Cambodia, 1975–79)

Pol Pot's programme aimed to purify Cambodian society of capitalism, Western culture, religion and all foreign influences in favour of an isolated and totally self-sufficient Maoist agrarian state. The country's entire population was forced to relocate to agricultural collectives, where an estimated 1.5 million were worked or starved to death, or executed for infringements such as complaining about living conditions, expressing religious sentiments or grieving over the loss of relatives or friends.

All these 20th century leaders achieved their position through their magnetism and stirring leadership qualities. In their name, their followers massacred as many of their fellow citizens as requested.

Perhaps they were driven to emulate the most influential and unforgiving leader of all, Yahweh (the Biblical God) who killed every living creature on Earth except for 6 people, Noah and his family, plus one male and female of each species of life. It is clearly easier to count the people who lived than the ones who were murdered.

WHAT WAS THE MOST HURTFUL THING A GIRLFRIEND TOLD YOU WHEN SHE DUMPED YOU?

he came up with some real corkers. "You have the IQ of lint, and the thought that terrifies me most is that someone may hate me the way I loathe you. What you lack in intelligence, you more than make up for in stupidity. Someday you will find yourself, and you will wish you hadn't. I worship the ground that awaits you, you snake."
I was so impressed by her withering review,
that I asked for another chance,
which she wisely
rejected.

She gave me a piece of her mind...

WHAT WAS YOUR WORST HOLIDAY?

n Summer 1986 David Puttnam and I were holidaying on a boat circling the Italian coast. Puttnam, an old comrade from the CDP ad agency from the time when we were energetic youths, both spotty and cocky in equal measure, was now a star movie maker with a Best Picture Academy Award for *Chariots of Fire*, and a portfolio of admired movies including *The Killing Fields*, *The Mission* and *The Duellists*. I got to enjoy few of the delights of Portofino and the Cinque Terre.

Puttnam was about to join Columbia Pictures as its Chief Exec, and had to green light 10 scripts for production (excuse me, approve), from the 150 that he had brought along in a large suitcase. He was expected to have his selection ready for his first day, Sept 1st, and I was expected to read the scripts and help him come up with the final choice.

On the last day of my supposed holiday, he summoned me to deliver my views. I had ploughed through them all, I confirmed, and thought they all stank. When he pressed me, I gingerly held up, with two fingers, one hopeful effort produced by Dick Clement and Ian La Frenais, two good writers (*Porridge*, *The Likely Lads* etc).

"This one, *Vice Versa*, is quite amusing", I offered, "but sadly the plot line (a father and son who magically enter each other's bodies) is too similar to a movie from a couple of years ago, *All of Me*, starring Steve Martin, with Lily Tomlin's soul accidentally entering his body." Before I could finish my little dissertation, I was firmly put in my place, reminded I knew nothing about the movie business, that

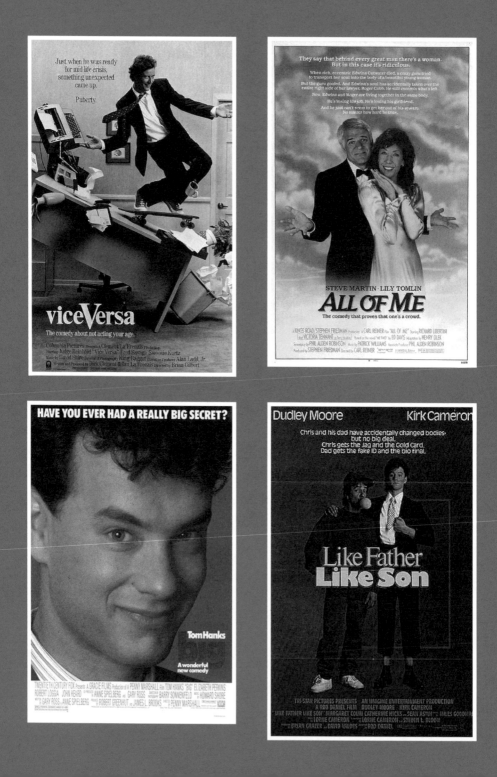

All of Me was a minor cult hit, but that *Vice Versa* had a much broader family appeal and would deliver a box office smash. Puttnam was of course right, and wrong.

There was to be a film with a 13 year-old transforming into a 35 year-old's body, it would be called *Big* and when it was released 2 years later it proved a global blockbuster.

Vice Versa, like the other 9 films David had to shine his green torch upon, faded without trace at the box office. (It wasn't helped that in one of those strange Hollywood co-incidences, a dull film called *Like Father Like Son* starring Dudley Moore, was released at the same time and it too featured a father and son swapping bodies.)

Puttnam also had the misfortune to pick a fight with the wrong people in Hollywood, almost as soon as he landed in town. He began with Michael Ovitz, boss of CAA, the most powerful agent in the movie world, and creator of the Package, whereby his agency, which represented most of the leading actors, directors, screenwriters would bundle up irresistible projects for the Studios, using their A+ client base.

David didn't approve of Agent Power, and also took on some of L.A.'s most successful and voluble producers, and got given a torrid time, until Columbia was bought by Sony, and he was presented with a munificent golden handshake.

He came back to Britain, became a peer and Lord Puttnam is now a fire-brand of the political world. No longer spotty, but I trust as cocky as ever, like me.

I
WHAT DID YOUR PARENTS TEACH YOU, THAT YOU REALIZED WAS TRUE?
II
IS IT CORRECT THAT BECAUSE YOUR FAMILY NAME IN ARABIC MEANS WATCH, THAT YOU CAME FROM A FAMILY OF WATCHMAKERS?

I

They convinced me that everything would be OK even though I was a disappointing child.

II

No watchmakers in the family I know of, though it would be nice if my great-granny invented Rolex and that I inherited the business.

WHAT IS THE ONE THING YOU WOULD NEVER, EVER WANT TO DO AGAIN IN YOUR LIFE?

Wet my bed.

WHAT IS THE MOST VALUABLE LIFE LESSON YOU CAN OFFER?

Eat a live toad first thing in the morning and nothing worse will happen to you all day.

HOW DO YOU FEEL ABOUT WOMEN WHO WEAR FUR?

 eople are more violently opposed to fur than leather because it's safer to harass rich women than a motorcycle gang.

HOW WOULD OTHERS DESCRIBE YOU?

He's the kind of person who lights up a room by flicking a switch.

IS BAD LUCK OFTEN A CASE OF STUPIDITY?

 n New York in 1977, a man was knocked down by a car, and got up uninjured. But a bystander suggested he feign injury, lay back down in front of the car, in order to collect an insurance claim. The car rolled forward and crushed him to death. Unlucky? Or stupid? Greed can ensure both.

Bad luck comes in many forms.

Unfortunate underground parking.

I HAVE GOT MY BOSS AND HIS WIFE COMING OVER FOR DINNER. HE IS A BIT OF A TECH-GEEK, AND THE WIFE LIKES TAKING HIM TO AFRICA FOR SAFARIS. THEY ARE BOTH A LITTLE UPTIGHT, SO HOW CAN I BREAK THE ICE AND GET THE EVENING OFF TO A RELAXING START?

 pen the conversation by revealing that the only country with more cell phones than regular phones is Finland, and that the elephant is the only animal besides humans that can stand on its head.

DO YOU THINK ADVERTISING WORKS GLOBALLY, OR ARE "INTERNATIONAL" AD CAMPAIGNS ALWAYS RATHER COMPROMISED BY CROSS-CULTURAL NEEDS?

Some hurdles do need to be surmounted in global marketing; these were some of the international brands that required particular care.

I HAVE JUST HAD A BUSINESS VENTURE FAIL, AND IT HAS LEFT ME POORER IN EVERY WAY, AND HAS SAPPED MY CONFIDENCE.
ANY GOOD IDEAS PLEASE, TO HELP ME GET BACK IN THE SADDLE?

I

Henry Ford had his first five businesses fail, leaving him broke each time, before he founded Ford Motor Company.

II

Soichiro Honda was turned down for a job as an engineer at Toyota, and after a long period of unemployment he started making scooters in his home, and his friends persuaded him to start a business selling them.

The Honda A-Type, Honda's first product on the market, 1947.

III

Bill Gates dropped out of Harvard and his first business 'Traf-O-Data', failed. He eventually started again with a new idea, Microsoft.

IV

Akio Morita's first venture for his fledgling business was a rice cooker, that burnt rice rather than cooked it, and sold less than 100 units. His tiny company, Sony, struggled but survived.

V

Colonel Sanders of Kentucky Fried Chicken had his famous secret chicken recipe rejected over 1000 times before a restaurant accepted.

VI

Walt Disney was fired by a newspaper editor because "he lacked imagination and had no good ideas". He started a number of businesses that all ended in failure and bankruptcy, before he invented Mickey Mouse.

VII

The good news for parents of children who don't seem overly bright is that Albert Einstein did not speak until he was four, and did not read until he was seven. He was expelled from school, and was refused acceptance to Zurich Polytechnic.

VIII

Thomas Edison was told by teachers he was "too stupid to learn anything". He was fired from his first two jobs for not being productive enough. Edison made over 1000 attempts at inventing the light bulb, before one of his ideas worked.

IX

Stephen King's first book *Carrie* received 30 rejections, causing King to give up and throw it in the rubbish bin. His wife rescued it and encouraged him to keep submitting it. He is now one of the bestselling authors of all time.

X

In 1954 Elvis Presley was fired from the Grand Ole Opry after just one performance, the manager telling him "You ain't goin' nowhere, son. You ought to go back to drivin' a truck". He had his first number one hit 2 years later.

Most people only got to the top after scraping along at the bottom. Failure is very disagreeable, but the bitter taste of it is often the finest spur to claw your way to success.

HOW WOULD YOU ADVISE A GIRL TO MEET A GOOD MAN IN LONDON?

Stroll around London's art museums. You will encounter a fine selection of cultured and sophisticated men, worldly, open to new ideas, and to meeting new friends wishing to discuss the works on display. I recommend the Saatchi Gallery, King's Rd, London SW3 in particular, for its consistent standard of highly attractive and intelligent visitors.

I'M CURRENTLY SEEING A PLEASANT CHAP, ALSO CALLED CHARLES BY THE WAY. HE SEEMS FAIRLY DECENT, HOWEVER HE HAS A WANDERING EYE. I ACCEPT THAT MOST PEOPLE DO, BUT MY ONLY REQUEST HAS BEEN FOR HIM TO PRACTISE THIS IN PRIVATE AND NOT IN ANY WAY NEAR ME. HOWEVER DESPITE THIS REPEATED REQUEST HE INSISTS ON SHARING HIS THOUGHTS WITH ME. I FIND IT OFF PUTTING, DISRESPECTFUL AND REDUCES MY DESIRE FOR HIM. AM I BEING TOO EXACTING? SHOULD I JUST SHUT UP?

He is insecure, and makes up for it by trying to make you equally vulnerable. Tedious, but if you embrace his character flaw in a more amused way, treating his wandering eye as a silly affliction, and need for attention, he may find your nonchalance more withering than your scolding, and actually grow up.

DO YOU HAVE A CLOSE FRIEND WHO YOU WOULD ENTRUST ANY SECRET TO, AND IS IT A MAN OR A WOMAN?

A friend is someone who will help you move home. A real friend is someone who will help you move a body.

DO YOU THINK THAT THE WARM SENSE OF
FAMILY IN MEDITERRANEAN COUNTRIES
CREATES A BETTER ENVIRONMENT FOR
CHILDREN THAN THE RATHER DISTANT
APPROACH TAKEN TO CHILDREN IN ENGLAND?
I prefer the British attitude to children:

WHAT IS MANKIND'S GREATEST UNSOLVED MYSTERY THAT PARTICULARLY PUZZLES YOU?

Why kamikaze pilots wore helmets.

~

Why do you hang clothes on a washing line
and not on a drying line?

~

Why does a fat chance and a slim chance
mean the same thing?

~

Why is it called a TV set when you only get one?

~

What would you call a burger made of ham?

~

If man evolved from monkeys and apes why do
we still have monkeys and apes?

~

How can you hear yourself think?

WHAT IS THE MOST HONEST GUIDANCE YOU CAN OFFER AN AMBITIOUS, STRUGGLING ARTIST?

Take my advice. I don't use it anyway.

PEOPLE SAY THAT TENACITY AND STAYING RESOLUTE ARE THE MOST IMPORTANT FACTORS IN BUSINESS SUCCESS. AGREE?

Tenacity and staying resolute are simply being obstinate in a way we approve of.

WHAT CAN YOU TELL ME THAT PROVES THAT RELIGION IS STILL OF VALUE AND IMPORTANCE TODAY?

Eighty-five percent of all weddings are held in a place of worship – an eye-opener to people like me, too unbelieving to be even lapsed.

WHAT DO YOU THINK WOULD CREATE WORLD PEACE?

Total nuclear annihilation.

IF AN OBJECT OR EXPRESSION CAN BRING ABOUT, WITHIN US, A SENSE OF SERENE MELANCHOLY AND A SPIRITUAL LONGING, THEN THAT OBJECT COULD BE SAID TO BE *WABI SABI*... IT NURTURES ALL THAT IS AUTHENTIC BY ACKNOWLEDGING THREE SIMPLE REALITIES: NOTHING LASTS, NOTHING IS FINISHED, AND NOTHING IS PERFECT. WHAT EXAMPLES OF *WABI SABI* OBJECTS HAVE MADE A LASTING IMPRESSION IN YOUR LIFE?

once had a 1967 Shelby Mustang V8 GT500. Electric blue. Preposterously fast. It certainly acknowledged your three simple realities. Nothing about it lasted very long, nothing in it was finished very well, and it was perfect only in a straight line. That's probably as close to *wabi sabi* as I have achieved.

WHEN YOU DROP IT, TOAST ALWAYS SEEMS TO LAND BUTTER SIDE DOWN. WHY?

attach my toast to the cat's back, prior to buttering. Cats always land on their feet, so the bread is therefore certain to land butter side up. But apologies, was yours a rhetorical question?

WHY DO MEN CHOOSE BLUE PAINTINGS?

o they? I had no idea. And I certainly couldn't tell you if I have fallen for more predominantly blue, or red, or green, or white, or yellow paintings. Maybe I'm too closely in touch with my feminine side, because I'm sure I have lots of purple and lilac around as well.

Blue is supposed to call to mind feelings of serenity, calm, a tranquil sense of security and order. Apparently, seeing the colour makes your body create soothing chemicals, so it is used in bedrooms.

But contradictorily it is also supposed to make office workers more productive to be in a blue-painted office, and weight-lifters handle heavier weights in a blue gym.

No, I don't believe this girly blather either.

WHERE HAS MANKIND GONE WRONG?

Putting an 's' in the word "lisp".

IF YOU WERE AN INSECT, WHAT WOULD YOU BE?

pretty juvenile question, which is fair enough, under the circumstances. A butterfly. I understand they taste with their feet, a sensation I would like to experience.

HOW CAN I TRAIN MYSELF TO BE A GOOD LISTENER? I AM ALWAYS FINISHING PEOPLES' SENTENCES, AND INTERRUPTING THEM IN FULL FLOW, WHICH MY FRIENDS SAY IS SIMPLY ACCEPTED AS LIVELY ENTHUSIASM. WHAT WOULD YOU SAY?

I would say that the anagram of 'listen' is 'silent'. When someone is telling you a story, all you can think about is that you can't wait for them to finish so that you can tell your own story that's not only better, but also directly involves you. That's the enthusiasm your friends are referring to.

Unless you are an orator of Cicero's abilities, simply get used to other people trying to dispense their favourite anecdote, while you are busy relaying yours.

IS THERE ANY FIGURE IN THE UK OR INTERNATIONALLY WHOSE POLICIES YOU BELIEVE IN, AND WHOSE APPROACH YOU ADMIRE?

WOULD YOU GENERALLY BE OVERDRESSED OR UNDERDRESSED AT A PARTY?
I don't much like parties, and it wouldn't help being dressed head to toe in Balenciaga, or my usual Selfridges number.

DO YOU REMEMBER YOUR DREAMS, AND DO YOU THINK DREAMS PROVE USEFUL TO PEOPLE IN ANY WAY?
I think if you want your dreams to come true, don't oversleep.

AREN'T YOU ONE OF LIFE'S SCEPTICS, CYNICAL ABOUT EVERYTHING AND EVERYONE?

ot compared to the third of Americans who believe man never landed on the moon. Or the people who voted Charlie Chaplin third in a Charlie Chaplin look-alike contest.

Or the government in India that once passed a law that forbade untouchables from casting their shadows on the upper-class Brahmans. But on reflection you are probably right; I was clearly too magnetized by Molière's *Misanthrope* as a youth, too seduced by his nihilist pessimism about the human condition. Is it too late now to mend my ways?

WHAT IS THE BEST BOND FILM?

liked all the ones starring Sean Connery. I saw only a few minutes of the Roger Moore and Timothy Dalton efforts. None of George Lazenby. Very happy with both Pierce Brosnan and Daniel Craig. They could try Timothy Olyphant next.

ARE YOU SUBJECT TO HYPOCHONDRIAC TENDENCIES – MANY SELF-ABSORBED MEN ARE?

I always worry that doctors call what they do "practice".

WHAT RIGHTS SHOULD THE FATHER HAVE IF HIS UNMARRIED GIRLFRIEND WANTS AN ABORTION?

None.

WHAT ARE YOU MOST PLEASED ABOUT IN YOUR-SELF?

My narcissism?

WHAT DO YOU THINK ABOUT PLASTIC SURGERY AND ANTI-AGEING TREATMENTS LIKE BOTOX?

remember a quote by somebody or other who was charmingly Pollyanna and optimistic: "No problem is insurmountable. With a little teamwork, courage and determination, we can overcome everything."

Sadly, I've left it too late for any team of courageous, determined doctors, or a multiple course of Botox injections to make much of a dent in my weary appearance.

DO YOU BELIEVE IN AS-TROLOGY? ARE THERE ANY TRAITS OF YOUR PERSON-ALITY THAT MATCH UP TO YOUR STAR SIGN?

'll say. I'm a Gemini, which I understand suggests a dual nature, a person who is unsettled, irrational, moonstruck, and probably schizophrenic.

Lorenzo de Medici, Godfather of today's
hedge-fund billionaire collectors

IN YOUR ESTIMATION, HOW MUCH OF THE LAST DECADE'S ART EXPLOSION IS DUE TO THE FACT THAT THE ART MARKET FUNCTIONS AS AN UNREGULATED STOCK-MARKET? (AS IN, NO RULES RE: INSIDER TRADING, GAMING THE SYSTEM, PUMPING & DUMPING...)

hen you say 'insider trading', do you mean museum board members getting early notice of artists about to be given wide exposure in a touring high-profile exhibition, and laying down a few works in advance? And do you also mean people who buy an artist's work in bulk, and then put up one of their works in a major auction, and quietly bid up the price, to raise the value of all their others? All very cynical, I'm sure. But the only people who get hurt are other speculators, who overpay, and end up with a lot of artwork of a transitory value that is unsustainable. My view is that anything that is done to promote art and artists, everything that broadens the number of collectors and visitors to museums, and increases the visibility and interest in contemporary art – that's fine and dandy.

Some people in the art world bemoan the hedge fund millionaires spending freely to festoon their giddily-chic designer duplexes with pictures, and driving prices to dizzying heights. Others bemoan art being treated as a commodity. But most of the bemoaning is because the art world is stuffed full of bemoaners, bemoaning about everything. Art collectors were spivvy and profiteering even during the Renaissance.

WHAT IS YOUR FAVOURITE SONG LYRIC?
Call me a drip, but here it is.

There's a saying old says that love is blind
Still we're often told, "Seek and ye shall find"
So I'm going to seek a certain girl I've had in mind
Looking everywhere, haven't found her yet
She's the big affair I cannot forget
Only girl I ever think of with regret
I'd like to add her initials to my monogram
Tell me, where is the shepherd for this lost lamb?

Chorus
There's a somebody I'm longing to see
I hope that she turns out to be
Someone who'll watch over me
I'm a little lamb who's lost in the wood
I know I could always be good
To one who'll watch over me

Although she may not be the girl some men think of as handsome
To my heart she carries the key
Won't you tell her please to put on some speed
Follow my lead, oh, how I need
Someone who'll watch over me
Repeat chorus

It may not be Eminem, but it's George
Gershwin at his best, an anthem
for needy types like me.

HOW MANY FOREIGN LANGUAGES DO YOU SPEAK?

 am too insecure to try my schoolgirl French, or my few snatches of German and Italian, unless it is quite unavoidable. My pantomime levels of incompetence make these examples of English translations from around the world especially delightful.

DID YOU HAVE A CLOSE RELATIONSHIP WITH YOUR MOTHER, AND HOW HAS THAT INFLUENCED YOU?

This photo was taken of me when I was 47.

WHY IS THERE AN "EMERGING ARTISTS" AGE PREJUDICE? SOMETIMES ARTISTS GET GOING LATER IN LIFE DUE TO CIRCUMSTANCES – BUT ALL ATTENTION IS ON "YOUNG" ARTISTS, COMPETITIONS ARE AGE RESTRICTED, ETC. ETC.

ld British Artists (OBAs) doesn't quite have the same zing as Young British Artists (YBAs). I have, believe me, looked at such a round-up of geezers, but it's not deeply uplifting dealing with crotchety older folk like me.

ARE YOU A GOOD DANCER?

haven't danced since my teens, sorry to say. But I obviously have tremendous aptitude, having won a jive contest as a gangly 15 year old at Butlin's, Clacton. I remember my partner was actually the dancer; she was eye-catchingly pretty, and such a gymnastic little mover that nobody noticed I was merely standing next to her, jiggling about with no co-ordination whatsoever. We won £20, but she never asked me to partner her up in any more contests.

IS IT TRUE THAT MOST ART CRITICS AND MOST ART TEACHERS WERE FAILURES AS ARTISTS?

ost artists are failures as artists. Either their work is not very good, or nobody very good has looked at it. But of course there is no such thing as a failed artist. The task is daunting and precarious, with very few achieving commercial success; often however, the effort yields its own reward.

IF YOU COULD COMMISSION AN ARTIST TO CREATE A MONUMENT TO SIT IN SOME NEW YORK LANDMARK, WHAT ARTIST WOULD YOU COMMISSION AND WHO WOULD YOU COMMISSION THEM TO SCULPT?

ichelangelo. King George III of England, who benevolently granted America its Independence, but remains woefully uncelebrated by the current incumbents of our colony.

HOW DO YOU FEEL ABOUT WOMEN GOING BRA-LESS IN THE OFFICE?

I see a problem here. Over a third of female lottery winners hide their winning ticket in their brassiere.

WHAT IS THE ODDEST HABIT YOU WILL ADMIT TO?

When driving and looking for an address, I turn down the volume on the radio.

WHAT LESSON HAVE YOU LEARNT IN YOUR YEARS IN ADVERTISING FROM THE SOCIOLOGICAL STUDIES, THE FOCUS GROUPS, THE RESEARCH POLLS, ABOUT HUMAN BEHAVIOUR?

129% of people exaggerate.

ARE YOU A STRONG CHESS PLAYER?

here are around 318,979,564,000 possible ways to play the first four moves per side in chess. I don't have what it takes to be even a very weak player.

DO YOU BELIEVE IN THE DEATH PENALTY? DO YOU FAVOUR LETHAL INJECTION OR ANOTHER OBSCENE FORM OF STATE MURDER?

e kill people for killing people to show other people that killing other people is wrong. You obviously feel fervently about this issue, so may I ask a question of you: why do so many 'last meals' on Death Row include Diet Coke?

Sulky teenager – sadly not mine. Mine are too edgy to pose for snapshots.

WHAT DID YOU GIVE YOUR CHILDREN FOR CHRISTMAS?

 badge for their blazers. "Be alert... the world needs more lerts." They didn't think it funny either, and demanded something more befitting their status as discriminating, elegant teenagers. But it's ok for little girls to whine. They are practising to be women.

WHO WAS THE EQUIVALENT OF "CHARLES SAATCHI" DURING THE RENAISSANCE?

I don't believe they had advertising agencies during the Renaissance, so he would probably have been broke and unemployable, as I was.

DO YOU KISS?

 assume you are asking if I adhere to the design principle "Keep it simple, stupid"? It is certainly a good idea to avoid unnecessary complexity in most things, and particularly osculation.

DO YOU THINK PEOPLE ARE TOO GOVERNED BY THE NEED TO ACQUIRE THE TRAPPINGS OF WEALTH, OR DO YOU THINK IT'S GOOD TO BE DEEPLY MOTIVATED BY THE DESIRE FOR ALL LIFE'S LUXURIES?

Most boat owners name their boats. The most popular boat name requested is "Obsession".

WHAT IS THE WORST HUMAN INVENTION? WHAT IS THE BEST?

 he worst human invention is Religion. The succour and guidance it has bestowed is far too high a price to defray the remorseless horror and bloodshed generated by religious conflict throughout history. The best invention would be football. Or possibly medicine.

WHAT KIND OF PERSON SPENDS £2 ON A FANCY BOTTLE OF MINERAL WATER?

Try spelling Evian backwards.

HAVE YOU EVER CONSULTED A PSYCHIC, FORTUNE TELLER, TAROT READER, MEDIUM OR CLAIRVOYANT OF ANY SORT?

Why do we never see the headline "Psychic wins £100 Million Lottery"?

The Fortune-Teller
a mezzotint after a painting by Sir Joshua Reynolds
(1723–1792), 1777

Eugène Delacroix, detail from
Attila and his Hordes Overrun Italy

WHICH OF THE GREAT MEN OF HISTORY HAD THE MOST DEFINITIVE CLARITY OF PURPOSE THAT INFORMED HIS ACHIEVEMENTS?

always felt Attila The Hun set the clearest path for himself, what would today be called his "mission statement". "Happiness lies in conquering one's enemies, in driving them in front of oneself, in taking their property, in savouring their despair, in outraging their wives and daughters." What he lacked in modesty (his pet sobriquet was The Scourge of God), he made up for in wisdom; he never attempted to take on Rome or Constantinople, instead accepting payments to leave them alone. He succeeded in devastating or annihilating everything else between the Black Sea and the Mediterranean in his short life, before he died on the wedding night of his 214th marriage. In Hungary, Turkey and Central Asia, he remains greatly revered.

DO YOU WORK OUT AT GYMS TO KEEP TONED AND FIT?

he strongest muscle in the body is the tongue, which in my case, as it is so opinionated, gets much rigorous exercise.

DO YOU SEE YOURSELF AS A GOOD FATHER?

ot compared to Ramses II, a pharaoh of Egypt, who died in 1225 BC. He fathered 96 sons and 60 daughters.

PICASSO SPOKE OF COLOURS MAKING EACH OTHER 'SING'. WHAT MAKES YOU SING?

Picasso.

HOW WOULD YOU DESCRIBE YOURSELF IF YOU DID NOT HAVE ART IN YOUR LIFE?

Bored, and just another rich dullard.

YOU SEEM VERY OPINIONATED ABOUT FILMS, BUT WHAT MAKES YOU SUCH AN EXPERT ABOUT THE MOVIE BUSINESS?

he hero can stoically handle the pain of a ferocious beating by a group of thugs, but will wince when his girlfriend applies water or antiseptic to his wounds.

His many opponents will have attacked him one at a time, waiting patiently for him to deal with each of them in turn. In any shoot-out, he will have survived being fired on by ten men, all ten of whom will be hit by his bullets.

When he is escaping from the baddies or the crooked cops, there will always be a passing parade (Mardi Gras, St. Patrick's Day, Easter floats, Carnival) to take cover in. This will be followed by a chase through a large restaurant kitchen.

The hero's best friend/partner will be killed off by the bad men a few days before retirement, especially if he has mentioned his family in the first few minutes of the film.

The hero will always have to answer to a Police Chief, who will always be wrong. If the hero is suspended, or given 24 hours to prove his point, he will crack the case in the allotted time.

The hero's new wife/girlfriend will be gunned down after the wedding or honeymoon.

The hero will have a small trickle of blood on the corner of his mouth or eyebrow, which he will casually wipe with his hand, and if it's been a particularly savage fight, possibly a slight skin abrasion on his cheek.

The hero will be divorced, but his ex-wife still loves him greatly, though she will not show it because he sacrificed his marriage for his crime-fighting work.

When the hero walks into a bar he usually gets into a brawl, usually under a Budweiser neon sign (product placement), and always if there is country music playing. He drinks his whisky straight with no ice in a shot glass, grimaces briefly, flashing clenched teeth.

The hero is always a bomb disposal expert and can identify and cut the correct wire, with only one second remaining on the LED visual display that an evil mastermind has thoughtfully provided.

The hero usually has to strip to his undershirt,
which makes him invulnerable to bullets.

The Supremes: the most beautiful
sound humankind has created.

DO YOU LIKE GIRL GROUPS OR BOY BANDS?

f you mean recent girl groups like Sugababes, Girls Aloud, Pussycat Dolls, Atomic Kitten, All Saints, Mis-Teeq, occasionally they make a track that's ok. But if you were enslaved by the mistresses of the genre, The Supremes, Shirelles, Chantels, Marvelettes, Crystals, Ronettes, Martha and the Vandellas, your ears are deaf and your eyes blinkered to the charms of the present crop. The Beach Boys, Rolling Stones and Beatles were all Boy Bands once, but nowadays it has undoubtedly become a term of derision, and nobody except grannies and pre-teens admit to finding their music anything less than emetic and feeble.

✝

HOW IMPORTANTLY IN YOUR LIFE DO YOU PLACE ECO CONCERNS?

Very. But what should I do if I see an endangered animal eating an endangered plant? In truth, Global Warming works me up into a frenzy of lethargy.

WOULD YOU DESCRIBE YOURSELF AS HARD WORKING OR LAZY?

I never put off till tomorrow what I can avoid altogether.

DID YOU KNOW THAT THE PHRASE 'RULE OF THUMB' CAME FROM A LAW ONCE USED IN ENGLAND WHICH FORBADE YOU FROM BEATING YOUR WIFE WITH ANYTHING WIDER THAN YOUR THUMB?

No I didn't. Why are you telling me this? Is it simply because I live in England, or have you heard that I am a ferocious wife-beater?

WILL YOUR COLLECTION HAVE VALUE FOR 100 YEARS?

I may not still be around, so I don't much care.

WHICH OF THE SEVEN WONDERS OF THE MODERN WORLD HAVE YOU SEEN?

 can't remember what they all are, but one of them must certainly have been the Diving Horses of Atlantic City. They started in 1905, and ended in 1978. The horses dove with girl jockeys from a 40 foot tower into a 12 foot deep tank. I wanted to have a go myself, but the girl-only jockey policy was a firm one, and in any event I am very scared of horses.

WHAT ARE YOUR THOUGHTS ON THE FOLLOWING STATEMENT: THAT HAPPINESS IN OUR CURRENT CONSUMERIST-CAPITALIST CULTURE RESTS ON INDIFFERENCE?

This reads like a question set in a Sociology examination, which I would have failed. For what it's worth, I think that if you cannot find happiness because you are constantly overwhelmed by the relative misfortune of others, then you are simply not sufficiently grateful for your own good fortune. As an example, it doesn't help the homeless feel any better knowing that people with a roof over their heads don't appreciate it. They might consider that in itself to be indifference.

HAVE YOU EVER BEEN SWIMMING WITH SHARKS?

Outside of the art world, you mean? I can't swim very elegantly and seldom take a dip, but I am more afraid of spiders and snakes than sharks. Shark attacks are quite rare, and more people are killed by dogs each year than are killed over several decades by the Great White shark.

WHAT IS THE BEST ADVERTISEMENT FOR A USELESS PRODUCT YOU EVER MADE?

Corduroy pillows. They're making headlines!

WHAT CONSTITUTES SUCCESS FOR YOU?

Waking up.

I FIND SOME OF YOUR ANSWERS ARE A BIT DISMISSIVE, NOT TO SAY RUDE. ARE YOU ALWAYS SO INCONSIDERATELY BLUNT?

I certainly hope so. Being painstakingly polite is most often a pretext for avoiding confrontation, and not hurting other people's feelings. In fact, a zealous regard for politeness is most commonly a way to avoid anyone thinking badly of you. It is simply vanity.

I FIND LIVING IN THE UK A REAL DRAG. I AM BEGINNING TO THINK THAT I WILL BE BETTER OFF SOMEWHERE ELSE BUT WILL MISS FRIENDS AND FAMILY. WHAT IS YOUR ASSESSMENT OF THE STATE OF MODERN SOCIETY IN THIS COUNTRY AND WHAT ADVICE WOULD YOU GIVE ME IN TRYING TO DEAL WITH THE DOWNSIDES?

I like living in Britain despite its many horribleNesses. Italy, America, Spain are all delightful for vacations, but modern society over there has just as many downsides as over here, possibly more; unless you can find contentment somewhere more remote, the absence of your family and friends will be a heavy burden. They won't be around to help you cope with the frustrations, irritations, dispiriting reality of contemporary urban life everywhere. Steel yourself to overcome the grimness around you. If you are strong enough to consider moving your life abroad, you are strong enough to re-invent yourself as someone who is thoroughly resilient and positive in the search for a more fulfilling life closer to home.

DO YOU BELIEVE IN GHOSTS?

How else do you imagine most celebrity autobiographies get written?

WHAT DID YOUR PARENTS MOST WANT YOU TO ACHIEVE?

I think they saw the whole purpose of my life was to serve as a warning to others.

SHOULD GAY MARRIAGE BE LEGAL?

 All marriage should be illegal. It's a flawed ideology, with a miserable track record, and only gives comfort to the insecure and needy, like me.

WHAT SPORTS DO YOU MOSTLY ENJOY?

mostly enjoy most of them. I also admit to adolescent fantasies about competing in them all, rather brilliantly. Well, not the Bull Run in Pamplona, Spain, where thrill-seekers run alongside a pack of bulls through the cobbled streets of the city to the bullring. Pamplona's finest young men are routinely tossed and gored
by the very pointy horns of the
1,000 lb fighting
bulls.

This gentleman in the kilt appears to have travelled from Scotland
especially to join the revellers.

OUTDOOR SCULPTURE IS AN IMPORTANT COMPONENT OF THE ART WORLD, BUT CONSIDERING IT IS SEEN BY MORE OF THE PUBLIC THAN ANY OTHER KIND OF ART, IT GETS COMPARATIVELY LITTLE CRITICAL ATTENTION. HOW DO YOU FEEL ABOUT PUBLIC SCULPTURE?

I f you see a statue of a man on a horse, and the horse has both its front legs in the air – the man died in battle. If the horse has one leg in the air, the rider died later, but as a result of wounds received in battle. If the horse has all four legs on the ground, the rider died of natural causes.

I did actually believe these helpful guidelines to municipal artworks until I saw the monument on the right, Washington's horse holding one paw in the air, despite its rider dying of natural causes. In general, however, most public sculpture is fairly dismal because it will have been approved by committee, and committees rarely make aesthetic breakthroughs in the works they commission. And art is often seen as a blight by residents living with a big sculpture on their doorstep. The locals are often vocal in their complaints, as they were once about a Richard Serra installation in New York. In truth, although I greatly admire Richard Serra, I don't know that I would want a 100ft long 10ft tall steel wall perched in the gardens outside my home. After a while, I fear I might miss the views of the flowers and trees.

NOW THAT YOU ARE IN YOUR SIXTIES, WHAT ARE THE TELL-TALE SIGNS THAT AGE HAS CREPT UP ON YOU?

Your back goes out more than you do. Your knees buckle but your belt won't. Everything hurts, and what doesn't hurt, doesn't work.

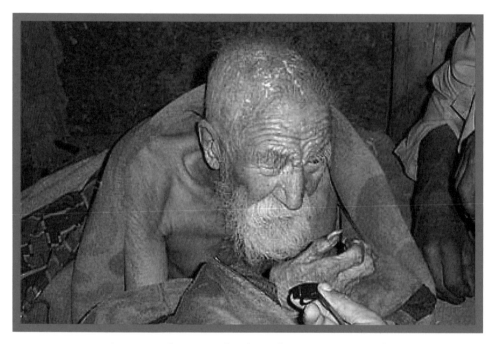

A recent photograph of me, being interviewed
for *Newsnight Review*

DO YOU AGREE THAT IT'S LONDON'S PARKS THAT MAKE IT THE MOST LOVELY BIG CITY IN THE WORLD?

f course I do, even though every year, London parks are doused in one million gallons of dog urine.

I HEARD THAT YOU READ ALL THE NEWSPAPERS EVERY DAY. WHAT'S YOUR FAVOURITE EVER HEADLINE?

egg Heads Arms Body. Sir Thomas Legg's appointment in 1999 to lead an inquiry into sales of arms to Sierra Leone.

I THINK YOU ARE A CHAR-LATAN, AND SHOULD BE PROSECUTED FOR THE DE-GRADED, AND BLASPHE-MOUS ARTWORK YOU INFLICT ON THE PUBLIC. PEOPLE WOULD LIKE TO SEE THE PERVERTED ART-ISTS YOU PONTIFICATE AND BRAG ABOUT LEFT TO ROT. HAVE YOU ANYTHING TO SAY IN DEFENCE?
I can do some soul-searching, but fear I won't find one.

CAN YOU DESCRIBE YOUR JOB IN ONE SENTENCE?
Exhilarating.

WHO HAS BEEN YOUR BIG-GEST INFLUENCE?
Jesus, obviously. And Stalin.

DO YOU ADMIT TO BEING BIG-HEADED AND SELF-IMPORTANT?

ot when I remember that our galaxy, which has billions of stars and planets, is merely one of a hundred billion other known galaxies. That fact should give anyone, even me, pause to reflect upon their own paltry insignificance.

ARE YOU RARELY OR OFTEN NOSTALGIC?
It's difficult to be nostalgic when you can't remember much of anything.

A COLLEAGUE AT WORK THINKS HE IS THE CAT'S WHISKERS, ALWAYS TRYING TO STEAL THE CREDIT FOR IDEAS THAT GO DOWN WELL, AND TRYING TO STAND OUT AND BE 'THE SPECIAL ONE'. WHAT WOULD YOU DO?

othing. Remember, the average person thinks he isn't. If you don't interrupt your enemy when he is making a miscalculation, he will make his own undoing.

WHAT'S THE MOST BITING CRITICISM SOMEONE HAS MADE ABOUT YOU, THAT YOU KNOW IS PAINFULLY ACCURATE?
He's alright in his own way, as long as he always gets it.

DID POETRY INFLUENCE YOU AT SOME SPECIAL TIME, DOES POETRY INFLUENCE YOU NOW?

ore people write poetry than read poetry. Personally I find it cringe-making to imagine the vaunting levels of self-absorption and self-regard required by poets. You need a higher degree of narcissism than even I possess to want your efforts disseminated.

DIDN'T I READ THAT YOU HAD A PET DOG THAT YOU TOOK TO YOUR ADVERTISING OF-FICE? I TAKE IT YOU PREFER DOGS TO CATS?

like dogs, but fear I relate too intimately with their soppy-eyed neediness, finding it oddly uplifting to watch them bolt frantically around the park, in a transport of ecstasy and liberation. Dogs are also gratefully subservient. A dog thinks, 'Hey, these people I live with feed me, love me, provide me with a nice warm dry home, pet me, take good care of me... They must be Gods'. A cat thinks 'Hey, these people I live with feed me, love me, provide me with a nice warm dry home, pet me, take good care of me... I must be a God'.

WHAT IS THE BEST TV SHOW EVER?

y favourites are *Phil Silver's Sgt. Bilko*, *Match of the Day*, *University Challenge*, *Fawlty Towers* which I assume are everybody else's favourites as well. I remember as a child hiding behind the sofa, watching *The Quatermass Experiment* through laced fingers across my eyes, more deliriously sick with terror than I could ever admit.

WHAT DO YOU BELIEVE HAPPENS TO US AFTER DEATH?

We are buried, or cremated.

DO YOU BELIEVE IN ALWAYS TRYING TO BE AN OPTIMIST?

I start looking for a silvery lining before I see a cloud.

WHAT IS YOUR POSITION ON THE CHURCH FURORE ABOUT PRIESTS AND YOUNG BOYS?

If you are on a diet, don't spend all day stood next to the sweet trolley.

ARE YOU A GOOD MULTI-TASKER?

have tried but multi-tasking for me means screwing up several things at once. I can, however, read on the lavatory.

IF YOU WERE OFFERED A KNIGHTHOOD, WOULD YOU ACCEPT IT?

Sir Lancelot
Eleanor Fortescue Brickdale, 1911

It is considered bad form to even hint about knighthoods or peerages you may have been offered, but declined. It's obviously vulgar to accept an honour of this sort, but even more tacky to refuse one, and then be a self-aggrandizing windbag about turning it down. It would have been a bit more meaningful once, being a Knight alongside Sir Lancelot and Sir Galahad at King Arthur's Round Table at Camelot.

DO YOU PREFER ABSTRACT ART OR FIGURATIVE ART?

Some people like prawns. Some people like snails.
Some enjoy both.

† Do I prefer Cubism to Constructivism?
† Do I prefer the Fauves to the Dadaists?
† Or the Minimalists to the Colour Field painters?
† The Impressionists or the Expressionists?
† The Barbizon School or the Ashcan School?
† Action Painting or Art Brut?
† Arte Povera to Conceptualism?
† Fluxus to Hyperrealism?
† Metaphysical Art to Primitivism?
† Romantic Art to Religious Art?
† Pop Art to the Pre-Raphaelites?
† Vorticism to Surrealism?
† Kinetic Art to Islamic Art?
† De Stijl to Futurism?
† Graffiti Art or Naïve Art?
† Suprematism or Lyrical Abstraction?
† Hudson River School or Tachisme?
† Pointillism or Mannerism?
† Blaue Reiter or Orphism?
† Op Art or Symbolism?

How fortunate am I to like bits of all kinds of art, mincing
my way round Italy's cathedrals, France's grand museums,
or a student organized pop-up exhibition at an abandoned
pie factory.

Barbizon School, Jean-François Millet, *The Gleaners*, 1857...

...or the Ashcan School, George Bellows, *The Big Dory*, 1913?

I HAVE DEVOTED MY LIFE TO WHAT CAN BE CALLED 'GOOD CAUSES', CHARITABLE AND SOCIAL WORK TO HELP OTHERS LESS FORTUNATE.

YET I AM CONSTANTLY BESET WITH PROBLEMS THAT BREAK MY SPIRIT. AS THIS PREVENTS ME IN DOING ALL I CAN FOR PEOPLE IN NEED, IT SEEMS ESPECIALLY UNFAIR.

Expecting the world to treat you fairly because you are good, is like expecting the bull not to charge because you are a vegetarian.

THE STORY OF THE GOOD SAMARITAN

DO YOU LIKE GRAFFITI ART?
Sometimes.

WHAT'S THE FUTURE FOR ADVERTISING?

 osy. More consumers are being created by the minute around the world, and the growth in regions that were unexplored by Starbucks, McDonalds and Procter & Gamble are now the burgeoning markets for America's favourite little companies.

All over the globe ad men are getting a little richer every day, you will be happy to know.

WITH YOUR EXPERIENCE OF POLITICIANS, HAVING WORKED ON SO MANY ELECTION CAMPAIGNS, DO YOU BELIEVE THEM TO BE HYPOCRITES?

 f only they were. Hypocrisy would mean they understood truthfulness, or even considered the possibility of sincerity. Before you can be a hypocrite, first you must have genuine beliefs that you can betray.

WHAT ARE YOU MOST
EMBARRASSED BY?

†

he hideousness of the contemporary art world. Being an art buyer these days is comprehensively and indisputably vulgar. It is the sport of the Eurotrashy, Hedgefundy, Hamptonites; of trendy Oligarchs and Oiligarchs; and of art dealers with masturbatory levels of self-regard. They were found nestling in their superyachts together in Venice for this year's spectacular Art Biennale. Venice is now firmly on the calendar of this new art world, alongside St. Barts at Christmas, and St. Tropez in August, in a giddy round of glamour-filled socializing, from one swanky party to another.

Artistic credentials are *au courant* in the important business of being seen as cultured, elegant and of course, stupendously rich.

Do any of these people actually enjoy looking at art? Do they simply enjoy having easily-recognized big-brand-name pictures, bought ostentatiously in auction rooms at eye-catching prices, to decorate their several homes, floating and otherwise, in an instant demonstration of drop-dead coolth and wealth.

Their pleasure is to be found in having their lovely friends measuring the weight of their baubles, and being awestruck. It is no surprise then, that the success of the über art dealers is based upon the mystical power that art now holds over

Still Life Of Wallflowers With A Mandolin
1890, Pierre Bourgogne

the super-rich. The new collectors, some of whom have become billionaires many times over through their business nous, are reduced to jibbering gratitude by their art dealer or art adviser who can help them appear refined, tasteful and hip, surrounded by their achingly cool masterpieces. Not so long ago, I believed that anything that helped broaden interest in current art was to be welcomed; that only an elitist snob would want art to be confined to a worthy group of aficionados.

But even a self-serving narcissistic show-off like me finds this new art world too toe-curling for comfort. In the fervour of peacock excess, it's not even considered necessary to waste one's time looking at the works on display.

At the world's mega-art blowouts,
it's only the pictures that
end up as wall-
flowers.

DO YOU THINK IN ORDER TO BE SUCCESS-FUL FIRST YOU MUST BE PREPARED TO BE SELF-CRITICAL?

I once thought I had made a mistake, but I was mistaken. Self-critique is a fine notion in theory, but nothing changes the fact that some days you are the pigeon, and some days the statue.

WHY IS FRANCE SUCH A POOR MARKET FOR CONTEMPORARY ART? NEW YORK, LONDON, MIAMI, L.A. AND NOW EVEN HONG KONG AND BEIJING ARE LEADING THE WORLD IN CONTEMPORARY ART PRODUCTION AND SALES. WHAT'S WITH THE FRENCH?
I LIVE HERE, MAKE ART HERE, AND CAN'T FIGURE IT OUT. THERE ARE TONS OF SHOWS AND FAIRS, BUT THEY JUST DON'T COMPARE WITH OTHER VENUES. WHAT'S YOUR TAKE?

rench artists are too romantic in a sentimentally cloying way, too mired in the glories of their past. They have been paralysed with insecurity since the birth of Abstract Expressionism in New York, unable for decades now to create anything sparked by the present day. Contemporary French art, with very, very few exceptions, is as irrelevant as their Johnny Hallyday was to rock music.

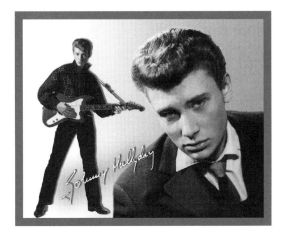

ARE YOU A BELIEVER THAT GOOD IS THE ENEMY OF GREAT?

his well-worn motivation-speak mantra is intended to spur people ever upwards. It is foolhardy nonsense.

Greatness is the preserve of the very few, and being good at something is an achievement that shouldn't be sniffed at. Many talented people become unglued in an obsessive/compulsive pursuit of perfection. The entire canon of self-improvement literature is of course reliant on ambushing our insecurities and inadequacies and propelling us on a fast-track to success and fulfilment. However ironic your reading of the advice on offer, it is touching in its optimism:

† You must remain focused on your journey to greatness.
† Don't wish it were easier; wish you were better.
† Don't wish for fewer problems, wish for more skills.
† Do not wait for your ship to come in – swim out to it.
† Success is not to be pursued; it is to be attracted by the person you have become.
† It is the set of the sails, not the direction of the wind that determines which way you will go.

Many of these invaluable guidelines, including *Good is the Enemy of Great* which was borrowed from Voltaire, are offered by self-help guru Jim Rohn, who helped himself to a splendid fortune by dispensing acres of motivational wisdom to hopeful Americans.

Fortunately one of his audience took a slightly askance view from Jim's, and wrote his own bestseller *How to be a Complete & Utter Failure in Life, Work and Everything: 44½ Steps to Lasting Underachievement*, which
I imagine was more spiritually
uplifting in every
way.

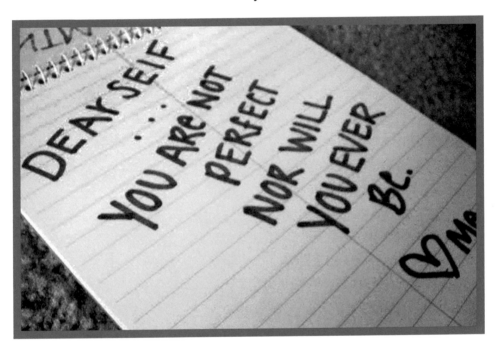

WHAT ADVICE WOULD YOU GIVE YOUR CHILDREN IF YOU SUSPECTED THEM OF SMOKING DOPE, OR WORSE?
Reality is a crutch for people who can't handle drugs.

WHAT ARE YOUR WORST FEATURES?
There are two things to dislike about me – my face.

ARE "FREE" AND "NEW" THE MOST OVER-USED WORDS IN ADVERTISING?
I have always puzzled about what is a 'free gift'? Aren't all 'gifts' free?

I HAVE READ YOU BEING VERY DISRESPECTFUL OF THE UNITED NATIONS. WHY?
Since the U.N. was founded in 1945, there have been 148 wars.

How I am seen by my poker opponents

DO YOU HAVE TO BE AS RUTHLESS AS YOU TO BE A STRONG POKER PLAYER, WHICH I HEAR YOU ARE?

 am laughably poor at poker. Indeed, I am a very popular guest at various poker games, because I am a predictably reliable loser. Poker requires, amongst other skills, patience. Good players are prepared to sit out many hands if their initial cards aren't promising. I am foolish enough to be intoxicated by the prospects of almost any opening cards I am dealt, and I continue to bet until my doom becomes all too clear. I'm not sure that great poker players are always particularly lovely people. Being the best they can be is often costly in the congeniality dept.

HAVE YOU LOST MONEY BY ENTRUSTING IT TO HEDGE FUNDS?
No. I think it's a good clue that someone who invests your money is called a broker.

IS IT TRUE TO SAY THAT WARS HAVE BEEN THE PRIME SOURCE OF INFLUENCING THE OUTCOME OF HISTORY, AND HAVE USUALLY ACTED AS AN ANTISEPTIC TO EVIL?
War doesn't determine who's right, war determines who's left.

CAN I BORROW YOUR LOO? WELL, ACTUALLY I HAVE A BIT OF A STRANGE IDEA FOR AN ART INSTALLATION, BUT NOT SURE HOW TO BEST GO ABOUT MAKING IT HAPPEN OR INDEED FUNDING IT. IF I GAVE YOU A BRIEF AND YOU LIKED IT, WOULD YOU (OR ONE OF YOUR TEAM) HELP ME?

 e have a fine installation in our restaurant lavatory, here at the Gallery; hundreds of bars of white soap placed floor to ceiling, creating a charming aroma. So I am sorry to say that the loo is occupied. I would nonetheless be happy to see the bit of a strange idea you mention.

WERE YOU REALLY AS HOPELESS AT MATHS AT SCHOOL AS YOU HAVE CLAIMED?
There are three kinds of people. Those who can count, and those who can't.

YOU ARE OBVIOUSLY A DIFFICULT-TO-PLEASE KIND OF PERSON. ARE YOU REGULARLY CRITICAL OF OTHERS?

 efore you criticize someone you should walk a mile in their shoes. That way when you criticize them, you are a mile away, and you have their shoes.

I AM A BELIEVER IN THE '3-STRIKES AND YOU'RE OUT' PRINCIPLE OF LAW WE PRACTICE IN THE US, ON THE BASIS IT KEEPS CAREER CRIMINALS INCARCERATED, WHERE THEY CAN DO THE PUBLIC NO MORE HARM. DO YOU TAKE THE SAME VIEW OF THE JUSTICE SYSTEM?

 eeping tabs on what laws you are breaking is never crystal clear, but fortunately some legislation, though never repealed, is seldom enforced. I fear that otherwise, there would be more of us in prison than out.

I   It is an act of treason to place a postage stamp bearing the Queen's image upside down.

II   It is illegal to die in the Houses of Parliament or to enter the building unless wearing a suit of armour.

III   In Ohio, it is against state law to get a fish drunk.

IV   In Vermont, women must get written permission from their husband to wear false teeth.

V   In France, it is illegal to call a pig Napoleon, or kiss on railways.

VI   In Antwerp, it is illegal to wear a red hat while walking on the main street.

VII   In Oklahoma, it is illegal to make faces at a dog.

VIII   It is against the law in Scotland to be drunk in possession of a cow.

IX   In Florida, unmarried women who parachute on a Sunday can be jailed.

X   In New Hampshire, it is illegal to tap your feet, nod your head or in any way keep tune to the music in a bar, restaurant or café.

XI   In Wilbur, Washington it is illegal to ride an ugly horse.

XII   In California, it is unlawful to set a mousetrap without a hunting license.

Fortunately for you, and me, there are hundreds of other statutes that could have us imprisoned for life, but for the problem of prison overcrowding.

The publisher risks jail in bringing you this image

HOW DOES YOUR ART COLLECTION AFFECT THE WAY YOU WALK IN THE WORLD?

 t's been pointed out that I have always had a stooped, shuffling gait, taking mincingly small steps. Not very rugged or red-blooded, it seems.

WHAT WOULD BE YOUR LAST MEAL IN PRISON PRIOR TO EXECUTION?

†

or your last meal on Death Row, your budget is $40, and the food must be bought locally. So if you imagined a final banquet of Roast Pheasant, Dauphinoise Potatoes, Haricots Verts, accompanied by a glass or two of Château Latour, or even a shot of tequila – then pardon me. (Or not, in most cases).

I have some handy facts for you about Death Row, to bring up in conversation whenever you may wish:

12.7 years is the average length of stay on Death Row prior to execution, and you will be living in a specific Death Row cell measuring 6 × 9 × 9.5 ft.

You are in isolation in your cell except for medical reasons, legal, or media interviews, and other approved visits.

You may shower and exercise every 48 hours, but with no contact with any other prisoner.

Death by lethal injection is now considered the most humane way of killing you. However, it is apparently sometimes extremely painful, and some unfortunates have taken over 20 minutes to die, gasping for air and convulsing. Autopsies often show severe chemical burns to the skin. There are probably a couple of people whom you feel would deserve murdering, but I hope for your sake not deserving enough for the long wait for an indifferent last meal.

Swami Vashikaran

DOES MEDITATION PLAY AN IMPORTANT PART IN YOUR LIFE?

Clearly not. But I did check into the amount of time necessary to achieve inner peace, and it makes the prospect a little daunting for me. You are hopefully a more receptive candidate, so here's what you need:

You choose a Mantra, and I can offer you a sample here to select from, which you will repeat every day in multiples of 108. (Mantra beads are helpful in keeping track of the number of repetitions you have done). Do this each day and the Mantra will repeat in your mind without any conscious instigation on your part, outside of your specified meditation time. You are advised to repeat the Mantra at other times, walking, taking a shower, doing the dishes. Put yourself to sleep at night repeating the Mantra, and wake up with your Mantra. As your Mantra must connect you with the sacred, select one that resonates with the area of your life or quality you most wish to enhance. If you are not fluent in Sanskrit, I have prepared you some handy translations:

OM (ohm)
The greatest of all Mantras it is the representation of the Supreme Being. The past, present and the future are all included in this one sound. Meditation on this sacred syllable is said to satisfy every need and leads to liberation.

OM MANI PADME HUM
(ohm mah-nay pahd-may hoom)
For opening the heart centre and developing compassion.

GATE GATE PARAGATE PARASAMGATE BODHI SVAHA
(gah-tay gah-tay pah-rah gay-tay pah-rah-sahm gah-tay bow-dee svah-hah)
To go beyond all illusion to the ultimate reality of God.

SHIVO HAM (shi-voh-hum)
To awaken to one's own spirituality.

OM TARE TURE TUTTARE TURE SOHA
(ohm ta-ray too-ray too-t-tar-ray too-ray so-ha)
To liberate oneself from fears.

THIRU NEELA KANTAM
(theeru nayla kan tam)
To remove current karmic conditions.

OM GUM GANAPATAYEI NAMAHA
(ohm goom gana-pa-tie-ay na-ma-ha)
To remove obstacles that are standing in the way of your progress.

OM SHARAVANA-BHAVAYA NAMAHA
(ohm sha-ra-van-a bha-vai-ya na-ma-ha)
To brighten and increase the positive effects of everything in your life.

Good luck, go in peace, live long and prosper, and may the force of Vashikaran be with you.

DO YOU THINK AMERICA OR EUROPE HAS A BETTER GROUP OF ARTIST MAKING CONTEMPORARY ART, AND WHY DO YOU THINK THAT IS?

I don't play Art Olympics. The US, UK and Germany have the best art schools, so not surprisingly, grow the most sophisticated artists. But I enjoyed throwing myself at Chinese art, Indian art, Middle Eastern art for our opening year of exhibitions, and found enough work that was invigorating. There is always an energetic, but unsubtle claque talking-up Russia, South America, Japan, Wherever, as the next hot ticket, the new investment goldmine, the source of emerging superstars. I'm sure their reasons are completely patriotic and indeed, altruistic.

DO YOU HAVE A COLLECTING OBSESSIVE COMPULSIVE DISORDER?

My aim in life isn't so much the pursuit of happiness as the happiness of pursuit.

WHAT DO YOU LOOK FOR IN EMPLOYEES?

There are three kinds of people in the world.
† People who make things happen.
† People who watch things happen.
† People who say "What happened?"

COMPLETE THIS SENTENCE, "IF AT FIRST YOU DON'T SUCCEED..."

...embrace mediocrity. Perfectionists know only despondency.

ARE YOU AS DUBIOUS AS I AM ABOUT 'FACTS' BASED ON STATISTICS?

42.7% of statistics are made up on the spot.

IS CREATING SOMETHING PERMANENT FOR POSTERITY THE HIGHEST THING WE CAN ACHIEVE IN OUR LIVES, BE IT ART OR OFFSPRING, AND IF SO, WHAT IF WE FAIL TO CREATE THESE TWO ITEMS?

Most of us create somewhat indifferent art, and offspring. In most cases, not bothering to fabricate either for posterity would be more circumspect.

WERE YOU AN OUTSTANDING PUPIL AT SCHOOL?

The longest anything ever stayed in my head was an hour, and that was a cold.

Sadly, I never made it into my school sixth form.

DO YOU HAVE MUCH EXPERIENCE OF LAWYERS? HOW CAN I FIND A GOOD ONE?

 s you know, 99% of lawyers give the rest a bad name. Search for specialists in your specific problem, and hope you find one you like, or better, someone who very much wants to win your case.

WHAT KIND OF ETHICAL RESPONSIBILITY DO YOU CARRY AS A DETERMINED ARBITER OF TASTE?

 orry. I can't quite picture myself as "a determined arbiter of taste". I wouldn't mind being "a tasteful arbiter of determination".

I READ YOU LIKE SPORTS, BUT ONLY ON TV, SAT IN YOUR ARMCHAIR. SOME OF MY FAVOURITE SPORTS AREN'T COVERED ON TV. ANY FAVOURITE SPORTS YOU GO TO SEE LIVE?

never miss Toe Wrestling. The World Toe Wrestling championships started in a pub in Wetton, Derbyshire in the Seventies. The contestants lock their toes together, and attempt to force their opponents' feet to the ground. The organizers applied in 1999 to have it included in the Olympic Games, but the spoilsports at the IOC declined. Top players include Paul 'Toeminator' Beech, and Alan 'Nasty' Nash, who is the current world champion.

The Annual Worm Charming Championships are not to be overlooked. Held in the lovely village of Willaston, Cheshire, each competitor gets a 3 × 3m plot of ground and has 30 minutes to bring as many worms to the surface as they can. The current world record was established on June 29th 2009 by Sophie Smith, who raised 567 worms.

What would June be without the World Stinging Nettle Challenge held in Marshwood, Dorset?

As you can probably deduce, competitors have to eat as many stinging nettles as possible in an hour. The contest has separate men's and women's sections and both current champions managed to consume 48ft of nettles.

All of these sports would clearly make superb television, but sadly do not make the schedules.

I HATE CALL CENTRES WHO CAN NEVER HELP YOU, AND ARE OFTEN THE OTHER SIDE OF THE WORLD. DO YOU HAVE REAL PEOPLE ANSWERING VISITOR CALLS AT THE SAATCHI GALLERY?

We do. But can you imagine what life is like for someone manning a busy call centre? This dialogue was recorded on the WordSure Customer Support line, where all calls are monitored.

†

OPERATOR Neil Page, computer assistance; may I help you?

CALLER Yes, well, I'm having trouble with WordSure.

O What sort of trouble?

C Well, I was just typing along, and all of a sudden the words went away.

O Went away?

C They disappeared.

O Hmm. So what does your screen look like now?

C Nothing.

O Nothing?

C It's blank; it won't accept anything when I type.

O Are you still in WordSure, or did you get out?

C How do I tell?

O Can you see the C: prompt on the screen?

C What's a sea-prompt?

O Never mind, can you move your cursor around the screen?

C There isn't any cursor: I told you, it won't accept anything I type.

O Does your monitor have a power indicator?

C What's a monitor?

O It's the thing with the screen on it that looks like a TV. Does it have a little light that tells you when it's on?

C I don't know.

O Well, then look on the back of the monitor and find where the power cord goes into it. Can you see that?

C Yes, I think so.

O Great. Follow the cord to the plug, and tell me if it's plugged into the wall.

C Yes, it is.

O When you were behind the monitor, did you notice that there were two cables plugged into the back of it, not just one?

C No.

O Well, there are. I need you to look back there again and find the other cable.

C Okay, here it is.

O Follow it for me, and tell me if it's plugged securely into the back of your computer.

C I can't reach.

O Uh huh. Well, can you see if it is?

C No.

O Even if you maybe put your knee on something and lean way over?

C Oh, it's not because I don't have the right angle – it's because it's dark.

O Dark?

C Yes – the office light is off, and the only light I have is coming in from the window.

O Well, turn on the office light then.

C I can't.

O No? Why not?

C Because there's a power failure.

O A power... A power failure? Aha, Okay, we've got it licked now. Do you still have the boxes and manuals and packing stuff your computer came in?

C Well, yes, I keep them in the closet.

O Good. Go get them, and unplug your system and pack it up just like it was when you got it. Then take it back to the store you bought it from.'

C Really? Is it that bad?

O Yes, I'm afraid it is.

C Well, all right then, I suppose. What do I tell them?

O Tell them you're too fucking stupid to own a computer.

Of course, the call centre promptly fired the employee, whom I'm sure you'll agree was exceptionally patient and helpful.

I AM SOMETIMES EASILY DRAWN INTO HEATED ARGUMENTS AND EVEN FULL-BLOWN FEUDS, BECAUSE I FIND IT DIFFICULT TO COMPROMISE. I HEAR YOU ARE UNCOMPROMISING AS WELL, AM I RIGHT? SO ANY ADVICE?

Compromise is the art of dividing a cake in such a way that everybody believes they get the biggest piece.

I HAVE HEARD THAT YOU ARE DISMISSIVE OF DEMOCRATIC DECISIONS MADE AT BOARD MEETINGS, AND REFUSED TO ATTEND ANY. SURELY THIS IS PLAIN ARROGANCE, FEELING YOURSELF SUPERIOR?

You're right, of course. But then, committees are often made up of individuals who can't do anything individually, who together decide there is nothing to be done.

WHAT'S THE GREATEST LESSON LIFE HAS TAUGHT YOU?

If you don't adore yourself unconditionally, why should anyone else? However deeply unappealing you may be, there will be somebody somewhere who finds you simply wonderful. How else would humankind have kept endlessly renewing itself?

PEOPLE USUALLY DON'T RESPOND WELL TO CONTEMPORARY ART. WHY DO YOU BELIEVE THAT IS?

†

he distinguished Russian artists Komar & Melamid decided to interpret a market research survey about aesthetic preferences and taste in painting. In 1995 they created America's Most Wanted & America's Most Unwanted paintings.

The survey asked peoples' favourite colour, second favourite colour, preference for outdoor or indoor scenes, religious or non-religious theme, preference for representation of reality or imaginary subject, hard angles or soft curves, vibrant palette or darker shades, preference for geometric or random patterns, wild animals or domestic, older or newer objects for the home, preference for complex images or simple images, preference for children, men or women, figures working, at leisure or posed, one person or a group, nude, partially or fully clothed, historical or celebrated people, ordinary people or famous contemporary people. Etc etc...

The list of questions was exhaustive, and enabled the artists to create the works that the survey decreed would best offer an accurate reflection of what Americans want their paintings to look like, and what they don't want them to look like.

Behold:

Komar & Melamid *America's Most Wanted*

Komar & Melamid *America's Most Unwanted*

Perhaps you would care to see the works produced in other
countries, where the identical research was continued:

Komar & Melamid *China's Most Wanted*

Komar & Melamid *China's Most Unwanted*

Komar & Melamid *Germany's Most Wanted*

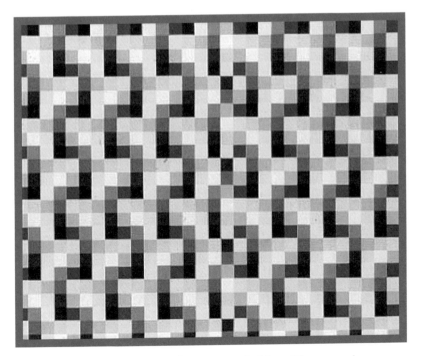

Komar & Melamid *Germany's Most Unwanted*

I SAW YOUR ANSWER TO A QUESTION ABOUT GLOBAL WARMING WHICH DEMONSTRATED HOW PEOPLE LIKE YOU CAN'T FACE THE FACTS ABOUT THE MAN-MADE DESTRUCTION OF OUR PLANET THROUGH 'GREENHOUSE' EMISSIONS.
WHY IS IT ONLY GLOBAL CORPORATIONS AND THEIR APOLOGISTS WHO FEEL THEY HAVE THE RIGHT TO RUIN THE PLANET FOR FUTURE GENERATIONS?

†

 hen you say people like me, do you mean the great majority of scientists, many of whom are Nobel Prize recipients, who have no vested interest in going along with the global warming propaganda?
By vested interest, I refer to those other scientists, whose colossal research grants and data funding is provided by organizations whose profits or influence will be greatly enhanced by suitable statistics; evidence for example, of the desperate need to create wildly expensive and pitifully inefficient wind farms across the world, wherever governments are stupid enough to buy them and decorate their countries with them. Everyone would be more concerned about global warming, but
for a few small
facts:

I   The Earth was hotter 1000 years ago. Temperatures were higher in the Medieval Warm Period than they were in the 1990s. Britain is one degree Celsius cooler than it was at the time of the Domesday Book.

II   If we look at more recent evidence, the hottest decade of the last century was the 1930s, pre-dating global corporations' supposed destruction of our eco-systems.

III   Greenland got its name from the verdant pastures of grain and hay, which have gradually disappeared over the centuries as ice continues to encroach further.

IV   2008 saw the Northern Hemisphere enjoy its greatest snow cover since 1966. Ice is not disappearing. Arctic ice volume is 500,000 sq km greater than this time last year, and the Antarctic sea-ice is at its highest level since 1979. Polar bear numbers are at record levels of 20–25,000. Fifty years ago, they were 8–10,000.

V   Sea levels are not falling, and holes in our atmosphere are not growing. During some decades sea levels drop by 2 cm. During other decades they rise by 2 cm. Similarly the Earth's ozone layer evolves and fluctuates over the centuries.

It is man's ultimate vanity to believe that we are in control of our planet, which as ever, is commanded by the whim of nature. Nature is by far a greater manipulator of our destiny than 10,000 Exxon Mobil and their like.

NOTE

It's always worth remembering the Golden Rule whenever you see a newspaper headline saying something like 'Scientists link butter to heart failure' at Farrell University Clinic: the scientists, their research study, their laboratories have all been funded by the Margarine Marketing Board.

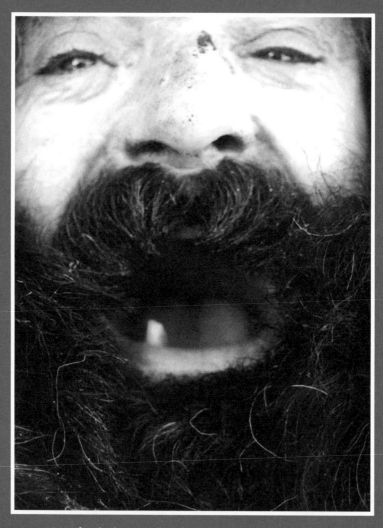

A perfectly happy, but homeless, Moscow citizen

ARE YOU ASHAMED OF TELLING PEOPLE AT YOUR SAATCHI & SAATCHI ADVERTISING AGENCY "I TRUST NO-ONE. NOT EVEN MYSELF"?

I cannot recall ever saying that. Nor do I recall that the person who did say it, Joseph Stalin, ever popped into the agency to give an inspirational self-help discourse to the Creative Dept. Nice sentiment though it is, my favourite Stalin homily remains "Gaiety is the Most Outstanding Feature of the Soviet Union", which I intend to pinch for the title of a new exhibition of contemporary Russian art.

WHAT DO YOU DO WHEN FACED WITH THE CHOICE OF TWO EVILS?

Take both.

I DAYDREAM A LOT. DO YOU?

I sometimes find myself lost in thought, and it's unfamiliar territory.

WHAT'S YOUR ADVICE ON DEALING WITH UNHELPFUL PEOPLE?

Try to never attribute to malice what can be adequately explained by stupidity.

DO YOU BELIEVE THAT MEN ARE FROM MARS, AND WOMEN ARE FROM VENUS?

Men are from Earth. Women are from Earth. Moaning about it won't change a thing.

IS IT TRUE THAT ABSENCE MAKES THE HEART GROW FONDER?

Absence makes the heart grow forgetful. Generally, the less people see of us, the less there is to dislike.

WHEN DO YOU WANT TO RETIRE?

At the crematorium.

HAVING SEEN SOME OF YOUR ANSWERS TO SERIOUS QUESTIONS, I WONDERED HOW OFTEN YOU ARE CALLED A MORON?

Things could be worse. Officially, a moron has higher intelligence than an imbecile, followed by an idiot.

First published in 2012 by Booth-Clibborn Editions
Reprint April 2012, Reprint September 2012
www.booth-clibborn.com

Text © 2012 Charles Saatchi
Design by OK-RM, London
Printed and bound in China
10 9 8 7 6 5 4 3 2 1
ISBN 978-1-4197-0373-7

Booth-Clibborn Editions has made all reasonable
efforts to reach artists, photographers and/or
copyright owners of images used in this book.
We are prepared to pay fair and reasonable fees for
any usage made without compensation agreement.

Charles Saatchi founded the Saatchi & Saatchi
advertising agency in 1970, which grew to become
the largest agency in the world. At the same time,
Saatchi started collecting art and later opened his
first gallery, a 30,000 square foot ex-paint factory
in Boundary Road, London.

His exhibitions have always focused on contemporary
artists and Saatchi's *Sensation* exhibition of
Young British Artists in 1997 at the Royal Academy,
London and at the Brooklyn Museum of Art,
New York sparked an explosion of controversy
about new British art.

The new 70,000 square foot Saatchi Gallery in the
Duke of York's HQ, King's Road is one of the largest
showcases for contemporary art in the world.

The Gallery offers free admission, helping it host
five of the six most visited exhibitions in London
in the last two Art Newspaper annual museum
visitor surveys.

IMAGE CREDITS

P.009 © Victoria and Albert Museum, London
P.021 © National Portrait Gallery, London
P.033 © Bridgeman Art Library Courtesy of DACS
P.034 All images © Disney
P.035 All images © Disney
P.038 © Scott King
P.043 © Victoria and Albert Museum, London
P.051 Robert Redford, Courtesy Rex Features
P.053 Harrison Ford, Courtesy of Rex Features
P.054 Russell Crowe, Courtesy of Rex Features
P.057 © Private Collection, New York
P.061 Bonnie Tyler, Courtesy of Rex Features
P.067 Courtesy Glore Psychiatric Museum of the St.
      Joseph Museums, Inc., St. Joseph, Missouri
P.068 Charles Darwin © National Portrait Gallery,
      London
P.071 Steel Dragon 2000, Courtesy of Joel Rogers
P.074 Courtesy of DACS
P.081 Courtesy of DACS
P.085 Courtesy of Rex Features
P.092 © 1987 TriStar Pictures, Inc. All Rights
      Reserved. Courtesy of TriStar Pictures
P.117 Courtesy of Rex Features
P.129 © Bridgeman Art Library
P.158 © Boris Mikhailov

The information in this book is based on material
supplied to Booth-Clibborn Editions/Abrams
by the author. While every effort has been made
to ensure accuracy, Booth-Clibborn Editions does
not under any circumstances accept responsibility
for any errors or omissions.

A Cataloguing-in-Publication record for this book
is available from the Publisher.

Booth-Clibborn Editions
Studio 83, 235 Earls Court Road, London SW5OEB

Distributed by Abrams/Chronicle books
www.abramsbooks.com

The Market Building, 72-74 Rosebery Avenue,
London EC1R 4RW